KT-573-651

Penguin Critical Studies
Advisory Editor: Bryan Loughrey

William Shakespeare

The Taming of the Shrew

Stevie Davies

Penguin Books

PENGUIN BOOKS

Published by the Penguin Group
Penguin Books Ltd, 27 Wrights Lane, London W8 5TZ, England
Penguin Books USA Inc., 375 Hudson Street, New York, New York 10014, USA
Penguin Books Australia Ltd, Ringwood, Victoria, Australia
Penguin Books Canada Ltd, 10 Alcorn Avenue, Toronto, Ontario, Canada M4V 3B2
Penguin Books (NZ) Ltd, 182–190 Wairau Road, Auckland 10, New Zealand

Penguin Books Ltd, Registered Offices: Harmondsworth, Middlesex, England

First published 1995
10 9 8 7 6 5 4 3 2 1

Filmset in Monophoto Times
Printed in England by Clays Ltd, St Ives plc

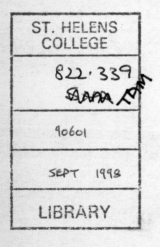

Penguin Critical Studies

The Taming of the Shrew

78882

Dr Stevie Davies lectured in English Literature at Manchester University from 1971 to 1984. She left teaching to become a full-time novelist and literary critic. Her novel, *Boy Blue*, published in 1987, won the Fawcett Society Book Prize in 1989, and was followed by *Primavera* (1990), *Arms and the Girl* (1992) and *Closing the Book* (1994). She has published eleven critical books, the most recent being *John Donne* (1994), *Emily Brontë: Heretic* (1994) and *Henry Vaughan* (1995). Her two previous books in the Penguin Critical Studies series are *To the Lighthouse* and *Twelfth Night*. She is currently Senior Research Fellow at Roehampton Institute.

Contents

Acknowledgements

My thanks are due to Frank Regan for all the support and encouragement he has given to the making of the book. I also thank Margaret Argyle, Monica Davies, Frances Hill, Andrew Howdle and Ann Mackay for all their help. I am grateful to my editor, Bryan Loughrey, for his understanding. I dedicate the book to four Katherines:

Kathy Gale
Kathryn Sutherland
Kate Turner
Katherine Wyatt

whose lives in different ways demonstrate the achievements of Kate *un*conformable.

For permission to use copyright material thanks are due to the following: Flamingo, an imprint of HarperCollins Publishers Limited, for *The Kitchen God's Wife* by Amy Tan; Macmillan Press Limited for *Recycling Shakespeare* by Charles Marowitz; Methuen for *The Living Image: Shakespearean Essays*: by T. R. Henn; The New York Times Company for an interview with Meryl Streep, 6 August 1978; Routledge for the Arden edition of *The Taming of the Shrew* (ed. Brian Morris); The University of Chicago Press for *The Meaning of Shakespeare* by Harold C. Goddard; and Michael Bogdanov for prompt book and Trevor Nunn for programme notes to their respective 1978 and 1967 Royal Shakespeare Company productions of *The Taming of the Shrew*.

Preface: Praising with Loud Damns

I could have been respectful. I could have been reserved. It would have been perfectly possible to disengage myself from my personal reactions to *The Shrew* in order to offer the reader a bland general introduction to the comedy, in which the playwright was congratulated on his technical genius, his capacity to amuse and provoke, his daring exploration not only of the sex war in the conflict between Katherina and Petruchio but of the illusory world of the theatre itself, through the frame-plot of Christopher Sly. I could have excused the misogynist excesses together with the dullness of some of the writing by observing that this was an early play, experimental therefore, a virtuoso masterpiece by the standards of the contemporary pre-1594 Elizabethan drama, and a brilliant piece of dextrous plotting and witty versification by a young Shakespeare. Indeed, I could have filled fifty pages with a discussion of the possible dating of the work and its tricky relationship to the play which was published under the title *The Taming of a Shrew* in 1594. Another fifty pages might have been spent admiring the technical innovations of the threefold plot (the Kate–Petruchio action, the Bianca sub-plot, the Sly frame) and the status of the taming action as a play-within-a-play. This could have led by natural progression into an interesting fifty-page survey of the different and often violent reactions the play has evoked, whether of praise or condemnation, rounded off by an explanation of how it is not really a nasty play if we view it in a historical light – or as an ironic attack on the misogyny it seems to reproduce – or as an exercise in multiple role-play that questions the reality of what it dramatizes – or as a harmless joke, a *jeu d'esprit* – or as a romantic and sexy comedy whose hero and heroine fall violently in love – or as a contribution to a Renaissance debate about gender and education – or as an example of Brechtian alienation – or as pantomime, farce, knockabout – or as ... anything you can think up that will save the Bard's face.

But does Shakespeare need either our obsequiousness or our condescension? Can it really damage the standing of his immortal statue at the centre of our culture if its monumental physiognomy is spattered with a little critical egg? Generations of critics seem to have harboured the anxious and arrogant fear that, if they do not support Shakespeare at his manifestly weaker points, that magnificent erection will somehow keel over and threaten to capsize on us. For centuries it was held in most quarters to be all but treasonable to suggest that the Bard might be less than word-perfect; that all his utterances, even the most absurd, pointless, reactionary or excrescent, might be less than totally meaningful. If Homer sometimes nods, it is also true that on occasion Shakespeare absolutely snores. Inevitably, even a cultural icon will have his off-days and even off-weeks; and of course the hard-worked dramatist, who was also an actor and shareholder in the company, did not have the benefit of knowing the posthumous glory ahead, and therefore lacked the incentive to revise for Immortality. Had Hemming and Condell not published the Folio in 1623, most of Shakespeare's plays would have vanished into the black hole of history. He was, in part, a hack; playing to the gallery for his living; collaborating with an acting company to pack the theatre with customers. It does no service to the study of literature to pretend that a mixed metaphor, a muddled scene or a corrupted conception which in another playwright would be discarded as just a mess somehow achieves sublimity in the mouth of Shakespeare; that his occasions of misogyny, class prejudice or anti-Semitism are less meretricious because they come outfitted from a wardrobe of beguiling words. Shakespeare himself was familiar with the disturbing power of beauty to gild falsehood:

> Thou mak'st faults graces that to thee resort.
> As on the finger of a thronèd queen
> The basest jewel will be well esteemed,
> So are those errors that in thee are seen
> To truths translated and for true things deemed.
>
> (Sonnet 96)

To resist the translation of falsehood into truth should surely be the primary duty of criticism.

In the light of such reflections, I have elected to tell my own truth about *The Shrew* in the following pages. Writing as a late twentieth-century woman, in the light of what it has cost women as a group and myself as an individual to emerge into public identity, I cannot tamely represent the comedy as a light-hearted romp nor persuade myself that its author intended a subversive critique of the values his plot endorses. Women endured centuries of purgatory to redeem themselves from the abusive attitudes enshrined in *The Taming of the Shrew*. Indeed, the plain-spokenness of Kate is our inheritance and birthright. We too are 'shrews' if this means claiming the right to speak our own truth:

> Why, sir, I trust I may have leave to speak,
> And speak I will. I am no child, no babe.
> Your betters have endured me say my mind,
> And if you cannot, best you stop your ears.
> My tongue will tell the anger of my heart,
> Or else my heart concealing it will break,
> And rather than it shall, I will be free
> Even to the uttermost, as I please, in words.
>
> (IV.3.73–80)

Kate's act of resistance equates language with identity: the bridling of her tongue will cause a breakdown of her whole personality as the pent-up pressure of unacknowledged rage builds behind the dam of repression. Rage is the story of her life as anger has been the catalyst to women's history. But whereas her voice is ultimately gagged by the hand of a man over her destiny (Shakespeare's) and the mouth of a man over her mouth (Petruchio's), her worst fears do not come about. For her world is a male fantasy. Her heart doesn't break. She is just reprogrammed. The new Kate speaks her tamer's language and he flies her from his wrist like a proud and bonny hawk, which answers to no call but its owner's. No doubt the tragedy of this 'comedy' is played out in many marriages. Wife-taming is no joke to those in women's refuges. And yet the play retains its enormous popularity on the stage and in the cinema: the auditorium rocks with laughter. Such laughter merits investigation. Does it incriminate or liberate?

The present book is charged with a strong antagonistic reaction against the ethics and politics of *The Taming of the Shrew* for which I make no apology. The play provokes and challenges its audience to engage with its issues. In part this is due to its excessive reputation, for the name Shakespeare acts as a kind of quality guarantee whereas the name Smith or Brown would release the work to stand or fall by its own merits. But largely, it is due to the fact that *The Shrew*'s subject-matter catches us on the raw by hooking on to the perennially fresh debate about sex, which no one can escape since each is condemned from birth to the fact of gender. 'It's a lovely boy,' cries the midwife, or 'It's a dear little girl', and out come the blue or the pink swaddlings to inaugurate our blue or pink destinies. It has been suggested that *The Shrew* sets one half of the audience against the other half; certainly it offers a comic challenge to female identity and a comic endorsement of male authority. Some performances will educe or introduce subtexts and ironies. Yet the surface stares us ruthlessly in the face, peremptorily demanding reaction.

Of the two options which seemed open when I began to write this book, I soon discarded the first: to damn it with faint praise by blandly accounting for sources, scenic development, characterization, themes, history of production. The solution for which I have opted is to present such information as scrupulously as possible, while also testing my gut reactions as a woman writing in 1994 against the play, carefully and closely read in relation to Renaissance and modern culture, even if this meant praising with loud damns. Standing back at a distance, I can see how deeply *The Shrew* must have 'got to' me during the months when I did little else but study it; how its whirling dervish dance of wit and fantasy provoked, needled, threatened, aroused – and amused. Asking disrespectful questions and hazarding perhaps controversial answers I hope may enable readers to arrive at personal assessments more freely for the testament of a critic who writes as a self-proclaimed 'shrew', a creature (so the *Bestiaries* tell us) with a shrill and disharmonious voice and a notably sharp bite.

1. The Tongue of Woman

PEDRO	Oh her tongue, her tongue.
JACQUES	Rather her many tongues.
PEDRO	Or rather strange tongues.
JACQUES	Her lying tongue.
PEDRO	Her lisping tongue.
JACQUES	Her long tongue.
PEDRO	Her lawlesse tongue.
JACQUES	Her loud tongue.
PEDRO	And her lickrish –
JACQUES	Many other tongues, and many stranger tongues
	Than ever Babel had to tell his ruines,
	Were women rais'd withall; but never a true one.

(John Fletcher, *The Woman's Prize*, V.2.36–41)

It was an incontrovertible fact that woman possessed a tongue of her own. But can she claim to possess a soul? Is she actually human or one of the lower animals? Does she sustain the capacity for moral virtue? These questions had exercised the minds of European philosophers and theologians for centuries, and were revived with renewed zeal in the Renaissance period. The matter of her intrinsic inferiority was never really under dispute: the tribunal of history had decided crushingly against her when 'our grand mother, Eve' had eaten the fruit of sin and passed it across to her husband, no doubt saucing it with persuasive words, so that all he could say for himself under interrogation was 'The woman whom thou gavest to be with me, she gave me of the tree, and I did eat' (Genesis 3:12). In all subsequent discussions of woman's nature, function and place, this act and its consequence (pain in childbirth, subordination to her husband who 'shall rule over thee' (3:16)) would be held up as conclusive proof of her infirmity or depravity. In 1595, a pamphlet was published entitled *A new disputation against women, in which it is proved that they are not human beings*: although we are told that it was a learned joke (see Maclean, pp. 12–13), such *jeux d'esprit* caper on the solid ground of communal prejudice. Most authorities agreed that of all woman's infirmities, the most galling was her incontinent tongue. Her garrulity was legendary, and apparently incurable.

'*One Tongue*,' John Milton used to say jovially in the hearing of his daughters, '*was enough for a Woeman!*' (see Darbishire, p. l). This was evidently considered by the poet to be a priceless witticism which never marred with the telling. Out of the various spellings available to him, in a period before spelling had standardized – 'woman', 'woeman', 'weoman' – Milton invariably selected the prejudicial 'woeman', or 'woe-to-man', recalling every time it was written down the fatal persuasion of Adam by Eve, which brought 'into this World a world of woe' (*Paradise Lost*, IX.11). By 'tongue' in this context, Milton meant 'language'. Although he taught his daughters to read to him in a number of foreign languages, including Hebrew, Ancient Syrian, Greek and Latin, he made sure that they knew only the pronunciation and not the meanings of the words. For '*One Tongue* [is] *enough for a Woeman*'. The jest masks fear and disapproval of the power that attends command of language, as well as contempt for female intelligence; fear of the female's desire to break free of restraint and to become even more out of control in Latin, Greek, French and Spanish than she is in her native English. The galled daughters looked on balefully. They sat and read to their father with greater or lesser degrees of reluctance and rage. At times, the patriarch's household echoed with their clamorous resentment. He farmed them out to learn various trades such as are 'proper for Women to learn' (see Darbishire, p. xlix) and disinherited them from his will, 'the unkind children . . . having been very undutifull to me' as he there complained (see Darbishire, pp. l–li). The Bard's daughters, like his first wife, had taken refuge in the last resort of the disenfranchised, the tongue. They were, in the discourse of the day, 'shrews', 'scolds', 'curst'.

Milton's etymological quip equating 'woman' with 'woeman' was not nearly as originally witty as he seems to have fancied. It was proverbial and demotic. In *The Taming of a Shrew*, the play that is considered to be a bad quarto (or memorial reconstruction) of Shakespeare's play *The Shrew* but may be a source or earlier version (see pp. 64–84 below), the equation is a central plank in Kate's culminating speech in favour of female subjection:

> Then to his image he did make a man.
> Olde *Adam* and from his side a sleepe,
> A rib was taken, of which the Lord did make,
> The woe of man so termd by *Adam* then,
> Woman for that, by her came sinne to us,
> And for her sin was *Adam* doomd to die,
> As *Sara* to her husband, so should we,
> Obey them, love them, keepe, and nourishe them . . .
>
> (*A Shrew*, p. 87)

Shakespeare's revision of this speech, omitting the letter of the biblical material, conserves the spirit: 'Thy husband is thy lord, thy life, thy keeper,/Thy head, thy sovereign' (V.2.145–6). Yet perhaps Milton's dispensation was more liberal than that which many contemporaries might have approved. The great misogynist at least allows woman *one* tongue. Public opinion in Renaissance England strongly suspected that one tongue was one too many. The best woman was either mute or spoke only in response to what was put to or asked of her, in confirmation or assent. Her language was a dialect of docility, soothing in timbre. Shrillness was much abhorred, and the assertion of personal opinion discouraged. The authority of the New Testament stood behind this premium on female silence, especially the misogynist St Paul's categorical instruction: 'I suffer not a woman to teach, nor to usurp authority over the man, but to be in silence' (I Timothy 2:12). Old Testament precepts in favour of the public and private gagging of women were also abundant, especially in the Book of Proverbs.

Much has been made of the so-called 'new woman' of the Tudor period, highly educated in classical and theological studies and influential in public affairs, and of the increased power and prestige of women under a long-lived queen. But Tudor 'new women' constituted a tiny minority of wealthy patricians. For every Margaret Roper, Anne Bacon, Lady Burghley and Mary Sidney, there lived tens of thousands of women without rights under law, property or literacy. Queen Elizabeth was a blazing anomaly, her red-gold hair echoed in the occasional flame of a powerful widow like Bess of Hardwick, in whom real (that is, economic) power, advantageous marriage settlements and the fortunate demise of a succession of rich husbands allowed a real voice, a 'say' and a liberated tongue whose word was law. An admiring biographer of Tudor 'women of action' (see Hogrefe, 1977, pp. 6; 41) records with a kind of rapture the fact that Mildred Cecil, wife of Lord Burghley, could speak Greek fluently and that her sister Anne Bacon, wife of Nicholas, mother of Francis, 'thought easily' in both Latin and Greek. But what was the effective use of these polyglottal accomplishments? Almost invariably in this period they articulate a complex form of suppression. Where publication was seen as dangerously close to unchastity – an indecent showing of oneself to all and sundry – and religious sanctions confined even high-ranking women to the private sphere, learned females who had penetrated the sanctum of male learning were constrained to ventriloquize patriarchal authorities. This predicament was ambivalently voiced in Elizabeth Cary's play, *The*

Tragedy of Mariam, which she took the risk of publishing, but as closet drama rather than as an acting script for production. Her heroine's destruction is precipitated by the same drive as launched the author into publication: the compulsion to express herself. 'Poore guiltles Queene ... /Unbridled speech is *Mariam*'s worst disgrace,/And will indanger her without desart,' complains one of Herod's Counsellors, and the Chorus follows this up by maintaining that the wife may express only one opinion (her husband's) and impart it only to one person (her husband): 'And though her thoughts reflect with purest light,/Her mind if not peculiar is not chast' (III.3).

For such reasons, women tended not to compose original works but to translate those of others: that is, they submitted themselves in the literary field to a self-effacing reproductive role, transmitting male texts. Margaret Roper's celebrated translations have been lost; Mary Sidney's surviving poems are verse translations of the Psalms into Elizabethan lyrics. Such labours delivered boy babies of the literary kind. Midwife to the word, these women, though much wiser than Milton's daughters, were scarcely freer to proclaim their wisdom.

Repression implies fear on the part of the repressor. Why should the tongue of woman have provoked such fear? In the Elizabethan and Jacobean periods, public speaking was an exclusively male prerogative, and rhetoric an important aspect of tuition in grammar schools and universities, since it prepared men for the professions by which they exercised government: as lawyers, judges and magistrates; Members of Parliament and councillors; schoolmasters and academics; clergymen and prelates, all exercised authority through the art of speech. Hence speech affirmed mastery in a hierarchical society in which the few were appointed as (so to speak) active tongues and the many as passive ears. The commanding tongue was a weapon which the 'murmuring' populace could envy but not appropriate. Mass illiteracy, which had operated for thousands of years as a means of class subjection, was challenged in the sixteenth and seventeenth centuries by the percolation of literacy into the lower ranks. Itinerant Puritan preachers and 'lecturers' would carry subversive messages from parish to parish in the seventeenth century, and were ruthlessly suppressed. Suppression encouraged rather than dissuaded the mutinous tongue. The Tudors and Stuarts penalized outspokenness violently. Women constituted an underclass on the one hand less threatening (since they were confined in fixed and separate households and were bred up for such confinement) and on the other more subversive, since their manifest and immemorial discontent brought the envy of the dispossessed to the board and hearth – into the very bed – of the paterfamilias. Ridicule and humour were then as now verbal means of control of the female tartar who sought to rule the roost. But, like all jokes, the joke against the 'shrew', 'scold' or 'virago' who wore the breeches and nagged her husband to death was a stratagem for dealing with threats potent enough to undermine the standing of a man among men by attacking the foundation of his caste, his virility. Kate in *The Taming of the Shrew* has to be 'manned' (a term from falconry with a strongly sexual connotation) so that her male kin shall not be unmanned.

Patriarchy's strength lies in its consolidation of all males into one community. Its weakness lies in the competition of these males for rank, property and the means of legitimate acquisition and dynastic transfer of these goods, through exclusive possession and use of the female. Hence, paradoxically, the female – nominally so low in the scale – has an unacknowledged power in legitimating the male's place in the pecking order. Although the law insists on her dependency upon him, he is dependent upon her to validate his patriarchal authority (see Kahn, pp. 13–17). A man with an unruly wife is only half a man. The male's 'honour' requires the female's compliance and fidelity: hence the prodigious body of jokes about cuckoldry in Renaissance drama. Success as a male depends on the ability to talk a woman down and to display her as tame to her master's will. The tongue therefore symbolizes sexual potency and prowess; it is a figure for the phallus itself.

This equation of tongue with penis is made explicit in Petruchio's first encounter with Kate in *The Shrew*. In a repartee replete with lewd insinuation, Petruchio builds to a triumphant climax in his wordplay on 'tongue' and 'tail':

PETRUCHIO Who knows not where a wasp does wear his sting?
          In his tail.
KATHERINA   In his tongue?
PETRUCHIO   Whose tongue?
KATHERINA Yours, if you talk of tales, and so farewell.
PETRUCHIO What, with my tongue in your tail? Nay, come again.
          Good Kate, I am a gentleman –
KATHERINA   That I'll try.
       She strikes him

                      (II.1.213–17)

The obscene innuendo in this verbal skirmish directs the audience's attention to the genital differences between the sexes and to the equipment of the male as against the openness to invasion of the female. Petruchio will pluck her 'sting' out of her 'tail'; Kate, having redirected attention from the genitals to the mouth (Petruchio's stinging, tale-telling tongue) turns her back. But in so doing, she has presented her vulnerable posterior to her opponent, who feigns to imagine that she has solicited penetration by his phallic 'tongue'. Kate has no recourse against this put-down but mortified violence, and slaps him, attempting to prevent retaliation by the reminder that a 'gentleman' cannot raise his hand against a lady. Petruchio's bawdy quibbles, in which he inevitably achieves the upper hand, depend for their victorious force upon the notion that in the battle between the sexes, the male is said to 'conquer' by 'taking' the female, who possesses no 'weapon' with which to defend herself. Hence her speech, however sharp, is not backed or guaranteed by that weaponry which is the male's biological inheritance and should enable him to subdue her in any quarrel. Kate's fighting is always defensive; Petruchio's invariably aggressive.

The civilized 'gentleman', of course, does not allow himself violent recourse to his physical advantage, and is therefore notionally open to disablement by a woman who refuses to acknowledge his superiority. But Petruchio is no such gentleman. His pathologically violent verbal and physical behaviour exposes the basis of force upon which the patriarchal system of marriage, the subordination of women and the ownership of property are founded. It is often remarked of *The Shrew* that, whereas Kate is credited with the capacity to sound off against the males in an ear-shattering way, in fact she only speaks 207 lines in the whole play, less than half as many as Petruchio, who speaks 564 lines and dominates the stage with a manic medley of violent activities which reinforce his speeches. In Act IV, scene 1, Kate is all but mute, and even in the earlier acts she is never permitted the flamboyant harangues which her husband-to-be enjoys. There is a curious disparity between the quantity of noise Kate actually emits and the hooliganism with which she is credited by her fellow protagonists. At the least sign of Kate's rancour, the males chorus their communal horror. Defending herself against humiliation by the suitors, Hortensio and Gremio, who have just pointed out that they would not have her on any terms, Kate replies that the feeling is mutual. However, if she did take on Hortensio, it would be her conjugal duty 'To comb your noddle with a three-legged stool,/And paint your face, and use you like a fool' (I.1.64–5). At this brave defence of hurt feelings, Hortensio and Gremio utter comically hysterical pleas for salvation:

HORTENSIO From all such devils, good Lord deliver us!
GREMIO   And me too, good Lord!

                                                    (66–7)

Tranio observes that the woman must be either insane or 'wonderful froward' (69) and Lucentio comments rapturously on the maidenly silence of the demure younger sister. The overreactions of the males to Kate's sullen pride (she has really said very little) are symptoms of mass neurosis. Later in Act I, Kate's clamour is mythologized by Tranio into mock-epic proportions:

> Marked you not how her sister
> Began to scold and raise up such a storm
> That mortal ears might hardly endure the din?
> (I.1.168–70)

Drawing on the mock-Marlovian rhetoric that Shakespeare's play shares in common with *A Shrew*, the servant compares the infernal girl's verbal rampages with an ear-splitting force of nature, committing a 'din' threatening to the very ear-drums of mere mortals. This outrageous disparity measures, of course, a *comic* gap; yet it also signals a kind of normative intemperance in the way males in *The Shrew* handle female noise. They either flee before it as from the devil himself, or go into battle against it by creating cacophony and confusion even more monstrous. Before we inquire into Kate's problem, we should consider what ails Petruchio, Hortensio, Gremio, Baptista – every man-jack of them.

The struggle in *The Shrew* is over possession of the word, as a sign of power and status. The language of action, volition and aggression is dominated in our common usage by buried metaphors of speech. For instance, we say that we 'assert a right', 'talk someone down', 'speak up for ourselves'. An order is given on the basis of a person's 'say-so'. Textbooks abounded in Renaissance Europe to equip men with the power of words. Hence the proverbial loquacity of women implied a covert project of usurpation. 'I would fain put off my last women's fault,' poignantly jests the Duchess of Malfi as she approaches her death, 'I'd not be tedious to you' (John Webster, *The Duchess of Malfi*, IV.2). If women's words were seen as lacking in substance, like counterfeit currency, yet words were in themselves potent. Words can literally change the world. Because change is always threatening to the *status quo*, the voices of the underclasses – including women – needed to be suppressed.

Words like 'scold' and 'shrew' evolved from this drive to keep the

...e in her rightful place. They are of ancient vintage, since women ...d from earliest times both resented their inferior social position and vociferated that resentment. Shakespeare's taming story is fetched out of popular folklore and ballad literature: it has not one definitive precursor but a body of antecedents and analogues, from the anonymous verse-tale, *A Shrewde and Curste Wyfe*, the ballad 'The Wife Wrapt in a Wether's Skin', Chaucer's 'Wife of Bath', Noah's wife in the Mystery Cycles and so on back into the dark antiquity of oral storytelling. The Sly plot, with folklore analogues in the tale of 'The Man Thinks He has been in Heaven', *The Arabian Nights* and ballads like 'The Waking Man's Dreame', is of equally ancient provenance, as is the romantic Bianca plot, with roots in Gascoigne's translation of Ariosto's *I Suppositi* (*Supposes*, 1566). More perhaps than any other Shakespearian comedy, *The Shrew* advertises itself as the retelling of a story that is as old as the battle of the sexes and a foretelling of a plot that will last as long as sex and marriage. Yet despite its enduring popularity, including adaptations such as Garrick's *Catharine and Petruchio*, a three-act farce which held the stage from 1756–1844, and the musical, *Kiss Me, Kate*, *The Shrew* has been a controversial embarrassment in the modern period. Shaw called Daly's 1887 production 'one vile insult to womanhood and manhood from the first word to the last' (see Haring-Smith, p. 69), and Michael Billington, commenting on the 1978 Bogdanov version, wondered whether there is any reason to revive a play that seems 'totally offensive to our age and our society' (*Guardian*, 5 May 1979). Words like 'virago' (from the Latin *vir*, 'man'), which originally implied the unnaturalness of a woman who aped a man by asserting her self, have been triumphantly appropriated so that women are proud to publish with the Virago Press, which has become an almost too respectable institution. To be a Virago author is to qualify as a serious contender for literary honours and prizes. Such a word, which was in Tudor times an agent of oppression, has become a site of contention. A virago then counted as a freak, a harridan, one of those weirdos spotted in the street by William Harrison in the 1580s, wearing 'doublets with pendant codpieces on the breast ... galligaskins to bear out their bums ... it hath passed my skill to discern whether they were men or women' (*Description of England*, 1587, in Hazlitt). An efflorescence of sexual indeterminacy also excited the Puritan Philip Stubbes to godly expostulations of fascinated horror at the 'hermaphrodites and monsters' who paraded the streets, at least of his imagination (*The Anatomie of Abuses*, 1583, in Hazlitt). But the Queen herself was a virago, the epitome of Spenser's 'martial maid', heir to the warrior-heroines, Penthesilia, Deborah and Virgil's Camilla, whose 'puissaunce' 'boastfull men so oft abasht to heare' (*The Faerie Queene*, III.4.1–3).

The conflict between the master-plot of *The Shrew* and the politically correct attitudes of our modern period throws into relief the extent to which the play's ideology derives from tensions and conflicts within the Tudor period itself, and especially the extent to which the social position of women was in the process of complex transformation. This coincided with the growth of Puritanism (see pp. 13–14 below) and the capitalistic upheaval that in the late sixteenth and early seventeenth centuries saw a 'yuppy' generation fight for the loot and lucre generated by a market economy based on growing industrialization and urbanization. Although the frame-plot concerns a lord and a tinker, opposite ranks in the feudal structure of inheritance, the inner story is set in the mercantile world of the wealthy middle classes, where mercenary young men seek the quick profits of grand dowries and old men calculate the sale of human commodities, their daughters, to the highest bidders. The price of a good woman, the Book of Proverbs tells us, is above rubies. A major objection to the shrewish daughter is that her value is not only low but probably nil on the money exchange. A sweetly silent daughter is worth her weight in gold. A sourly loud-mouthed daughter is a drain on paternal finances: her supply outstrips demand. Hortensio, however, is sure (and proves right) that:

there be good fellows in the world, and a man could light on them, would take her with all her faults, and money enough.

(I.1.126–8)

And although the aged pantaloon, Gremio, is sceptical as to whether any male will be found to whom Katherina's dowry could compensate for the nuisance of her company, the next scene sees the arrival of a suitor who is candidly in search of money with a wife attached:

> I come to wive it wealthily in Padua;
> If wealthily, then happily in Padua.
> (I.2.74–5)

This swaggeringly honest statement of intent works on a two-way bias in a comedy which plays off the romantic choice of Lucentio against the bargain-hunting prowess of Petruchio. The play honestly acknowledges the extent to which Elizabethan marriage was still conducted on the policy of material gain, with bargains struck between parents and suitors so as to benefit each party, without reference to the young woman's desires or affections. Gentlemen sought propertied widows in order to climb the social ladder: Hortensio, sniffing out Bianca's concealed affair, announces an alternative policy: 'I will be married to a wealthy widow/Ere three days pass' (IV.2.37–8). The blathering Widow accordingly appears in the final act. She represents the legitimate transfer of one male's assets (those of her dead husband and father) into the possession of another (the husband), and as such requires no other name than Widow. And of course, as it turns out, she too is a shrew.

The concept of the shrew is scarcely to be understood outside its connection with property, ownership and belonging. Petruchio's public declaration of ownership of his wife in the central act may be shocking to us and has led many critics queasily to conceive that Shakespeare could not have meant us to accept it 'uncritically' (see Kahn, p. 110). But it represents an accurate statement of the law as it stood in regard to married women in Shakespeare's period:

> I will be master of what is mine own.
> She is my goods, my chattels, she is my house,
> My household stuff, my field, my barn,
> My horse, my ox, my ass, my any thing,
> And here she stands. Touch her whoever dare!
>
> (III.2.228–32)

As nobody is seeking or ever has sought to touch Kate, except with a view to fending her off, the ultimatum is an ironic deflection not of society's claims on Kate but of her own attempt to assert her self. Can a chattel demand its rights? Does a barn speak up for itself? Do ox and ass command the English language? The speech articulates the Elizabethan marriage laws without elaboration or exaggeration. For a married woman had almost no rights. Possessing no civil or civic functions, she was debarred from office in camp, council, bench or jury-box. She could neither vote nor be a candidate, nor (generally) give evidence in a lawcourt. She could not make a contract, sue or be sued. The reason for this was that a married woman did not, in law, *exist*. Until the second half of the nineteenth century, a married woman was classed as 'feme covert', that is, her legal being was suspended as she was considered to be 'covered' by the husband, who must answer for her. Furthermore, she could not own property because she *was* property. She owned neither the dowry she brought with her, nor the roof over her head, neither the jewels, if any, round her neck, nor the very clothes in which she stood up. When Petruchio in Act IV decides what Kate shall eat (nothing), how long she shall sleep (no time), the quantity and quality of her new cap and gown (none), he obeys the letter if not the spirit of the law. For his decisions automatically subsume hers.

Throughout the taming, Petruchio ironically 'speaks for' Kate, contradicting her express utterances by repeating and endorsing them as if she had said the opposite. Through this device, he effectively mutes Kate. She is nothing but a ventriloquist's dummy:

KATHERINA Belike you mean to make a puppet of me.
PETRUCHIO Why, true, he means to make a puppet of thee.
TAILOR She says your worship means to make a puppet of her.

(IV.3.103–5)

Dressmaker's dummy and puppeteer's yes-woman (even when she says no), Kate is perceived as the cipher the law makes her as a wife, even when she defies and denies it. For Petruchio as her husband is also her guardian, and owns outright her chattels, which he could alienate (transfer ownership) if it occurred to him to do so. Hence Kate's spirited insistence on her right not only to make her own choices but also to have her own say is a delusion. Famished, short of sleep and taunted with handsome headgear that is then forbidden, she bursts out:

> Why, sir, I trust I may have leave to speak,
> And speak I will. I am no child, no babe.
> Your betters have endured me say my mind,
> And if you cannot, best you stop your ears.
>
> (IV.3.73–6)

But Kate is mistaken. In law she is precisely a 'child', a 'babe'. Her infancy means that she is without legitimate claim to a voice or a say; as the perpetual equivalent of a minor, her dumb status is as uncontroversial and obvious as the statement that the sun shines by day.

Because the social order was equated with the natural order, Kate's denial of her secondary status brings absurdly into question the hierarchy of creation, confusing night with day, chattel with owner. If she will not be dumb, Petruchio must feign deaf until he forces her to the point where she is willing to bring her logic to its most extreme point by confounding sun with moon and aged man with youthful woman (IV.4). Finally, 'kiss me, Kate', the husband commands (V.1.131) and a 'conformable' wife complies. A kiss will 'seal the title', that is, the contract, as Petruchio had pointed out in the central act (III.2.122), transferring all Kate's rights to himself – including her lips and tongue. When Kate arises into the spotlit centre of the stage in the final act and

ers her so-called 'great speech' in praise of female subjection
.2.135–78), at forty-four lines the longest in the play, her tongue has
been appropriated to her 'lord ... life ... keeper,/... head ... sovereign' (145–6), and she may safely be permitted the uncensored use of
her voice because it has been alienated from her to the use of her
husband. Through her mouth speaks not merely an individual but the
whole Elizabethan system of law and custom, which not only places
'your [women's] hands below your husband's foot' (176) but their
property in his pocket and their tongues under his jurisdiction. Whether
the play gives scope for an ironic and ambivalent interpretation of these
words and actions is a question that will be argued out later: for the
present it is essential to establish the moral and political basis of the
taming story in Tudor law and custom.

It is often maintained that the Elizabethan period represented a great
age of emancipation for women – often on the flimsiest possible
grounds, such as the reign of a powerful, highly educated and astute
queen rather than a king. Elizabeth, with her caustic wit, her multi-
faceted and subtle policies, her public-relations brilliance and her capacity
for ambivalent eloquence (see Teague in Cerasano and Wynne-
Davies, pp. 63–78), was however no more a rule for conduct in the 1590s
than Margaret Thatcher in the 1980s, with her all-male Cabinet and
her royal 'we'. Notwithstanding that the sixteenth century happened
to constitute a period deficient in male heirs, so that Mary Tudor, Mary
Stuart and Elizabeth Tudor all succeeded to the throne, a woman in
power represented an anomaly. Elizabeth's political capital deviously
rested in this anomalousness: she had herself represented as a miracu-
lous godsend whose violation of norms (refusal of marriage, childbirth
and the secondary status of a wife) was constructed as a singular act of
transcendence which confirmed those norms for lesser mortals. Although powerful female individuals did emerge in the period and
learning became a sign of good breeding in a female, the Elizabethan
period was not in fact a time of significant liberation. The conservative
ethic preached by John Knox in his infamous *First Blast of the Trumpet
against the Monstrous Regiment of Women* (1558), in which he claimed
that it was 'more than a monster in nature' for a woman to rule over
men, since women were fallen, corrupted and doomed to servility for
Eve's fault, ushered in a vigorous pamphlet war about the nature and
status of women. Knox's blast was retorted against himself by, for
instance, John Aylmer's *An Harbour for Faithful and True Subjects
against the Late Blown Blast concerning the Government of Women*
(1559), but such ripostes were not the work of feminists but of those

loyal to the Tudor dynasty and the Henrician Church reforms. Puritan assaults on the roaring girls of London in the late sixteenth and early seventeenth centuries demonstrate that some women at least were exhibiting a modish rebellion against the norms; a newfangled city culture, often revolving around the theatres and mirrored in the plays of the period, was creating anomalies: and noisy anomalies. Henry Smith, preacher at St Clement Dane's, reminded readers in his *Preparative to Marriage* (1591) that modesty in behaviour was to be accompanied by continence in the use of the tongue, 'for the ornament of a woman is silence, and therefore the law was given to the man rather than to the woman, to show that he should be the teacher and she the hearer'. That such reminders were deemed to be necessary certainly indicates the extent to which the 'monstrous regiment' was making itself heard.

But how large was the regiment? It was not until the early seventeenth century that under the complex influence of radical Puritanism, which at once subjected wife to husband, raised her as 'helpmeet' and friend, and imbued her with a sense of individual self and conscience, that women's voices began to break out into prophecy and polemic. Joseph Swetnam's vitriolic pamphlet *The Araignment of Lewde, idle, froward and unconstant women* in 1615 inspired five answers, three being by authors using female names, the best known being that of Rachel Speght, *A Mouzell for Melastomus, The Cynical Bayter of, and foule mouthed Barker against Evahs sex* (1617):

[M]an was created of the dust of the earth, but woman was made of a part of man, after that he was a living soule: yet was shee not produced from *Adams* foote, to be his too low inferiour; nor from his head to be his superiour, but from his side, neare his heart, to be his equall; that where he is Lord, she may be Lady . . .   (sig. D1v)

[N]o authoritie hath hee given him to domineere, or basely command and imploy his wife, as a servant . . .   (sig. D4v)

Speght issues out into the public arena equipped with a Bible, the self-confidence to interpret it for herself and a holy indignation against the 'Cynical Bayter' and 'foule mouthed Barker', her adversary. To read *The Shrew* in this context is to recognize the narrow constraints within which Kate's life and mind are walled. Her anger is unfocused, her consciousness undirected *save* to a sense of domestic disaffection in which her needs have never been met, nor are likely to be. Disgruntled rather than radical, Kate has native wit but no extended horizons. She neither constitutes a challenge to the *status quo*, nor represents a sign of the times.

Despite the rampant visibility of a minority and the Puritan insistence on companionate marriage, opportunities for action and self-development had in fact contracted rather than expanded in the Elizabethan period. Whereas some women had from the medieval period acted as sheriffs, churchwardens, Justices of the Peace, guild members, estate managers and businesswomen of all kinds, in the late sixteenth century men were extending their control over property, movable and personal, and the already minimal rights of married women to act for themselves and to will property, as honorary 'femes soles', were actually decreasing. Similarly the movement to educate women to become genuine companions for their menfolk was encountering a reactionary backlash, as the theory that learning increases submissiveness by reinforcing orthodox ideologies was met by contrary evidence that education strengthens personal judgement and the power to voice and enact such judgement. The theory that seems to pertain in *The Shrew* is that women are pretty well ineducable. Baptista attempts to increase the value of his offspring by affording them a classical education. Neither girl is susceptible of improvement, either on the Latin or the music front. The intractable Katherina smashes her lute over the supposed music teacher's head, enragedly refusing indoctrination: ' "Frets, call you these?" quoth she, "I'll fume with them" ' (II.1.152), whereas Bianca, outwardly conforming to the paternal desire for 'good bringing-up' (I.1.99) by application to her Latin books and musical instruments, exploits her classics lessons as a cover for amatory negotiation, and does just what she likes, when she likes, with whom she likes, just as (it is implied) women have always done.

At the end of the comedy, by a neat peripety, Bianca has exchanged roles with her termagant sister, whose taming coincides with the younger girl's transformation into a shrew. Bianca won't come at her husband's entreaty just as the Widow refuses her lord's command. Kate's subservient action of depositing her cap under Petruchio's foot (the cap itself being a sign of female inferiority, in conformity with St Paul's injunction to women to cover their heads) is met with a chorus of disgust by both other women:

WIDOW Lord, let me never have a cause to sigh
       Till I be brought to such a silly pass!
BIANCA Fie, what a foolish duty call you this?

(V.2.122–4)

She retorts 'The more fool you' to her irked husband's reminder that he laid a bet on her obedience and has lost the wager (128). The comedy plays out the proverbial shrewishness of all women. Tame one, and two others break out in mutiny.

If women's loquacity was an expression of the balked desire to dominate, what was needed was a 'taming-school' (IV.2.54) whereby the art may be disseminated 'To tame a shrew and charm her chattering tongue' (58). In Elizabethan England, female bellyaching was not only a personal nuisance, it was also against the law. The very title of the play would have brought to mind a wealth of folklore and communal experience, as well as the expectation of a body of easy laughs that accompanies the subject. The word 'shrew' is current no longer; nor is there in common parlance an exact synonym for either 'shrew' or 'scold'. Though 'nagging wives' are considered to be a bane, a 'nag' is not in the same position as a 'scold' because there is no explicit law against her verbal activities – save, perhaps, in the pronouncements of rogue judges willing to acquit a murderer on the grounds of sufficient provocation by his 'nagging' wife.

For the offence of scolding, a woman could be fined; confined to a brank or padlocked to a bridle; sentenced to the cucking-stool (from the French *coquine*, meaning 'hussy') or ducking-stool, to be immersed in the river or village pond, winter or summer. The apparatus for these punishments was provided by the local authorities. The suggestion sometimes made that the tongues of persistent offenders should be cut out was never actually put into operation. Punishments had not changed since medieval times. The typical case of Alice Stether, charged in 1375 with 'being a common scold' and sentenced to the pillory (see Amt, p. 74) is not in essence dissimilar to the sentence passed on Alice Crathorne in Kent in 1616 for being 'a common swearer and a brawling scold' (see Fraser, p. 103). Only a woman could qualify as a scold, legitimating the distinction between loud noise made by a male, a sign of manliness, and that uttered by a female, a sign of unwomanliness. The penalty for such tirades was to display the offender at the horse-pond or market-place for public ridicule. Kate's humiliations in *The Shrew*, dismaying to some modern readers and viewers, are a rollicking version of a common penalty with which the contemporary audience would have been familiar:

> She eat no meat today, nor none today shall eat
> Last night she slept not, nor tonight she shall not.
>
> (IV.1.183–4)

> He that knows better how to tame a shrew,
> Now let him speak – 'tis charity to show.
>
> (196–7)

Here in a rare aside Petruchio addresses in a voice of complicity the male portion of the audience, in the name of 'charity', that is, public spirit. For the whole male community is equally pestered by the equivalent of Alice Stether, Alice Crathorne and Katherina Minola. Ironically, he plays on the form of the marriage ceremony, in which the priest, turning to the congregation, solemnly requires that 'if any man can shew any just cause, why they may not lawfully be joined together: let him now speake' (*Form of Solemnization of Matrimony*). Either the audience holds its peace, for after all nobody has an answer, or various last resorts might be suggested. The implication is that most husbands have unconformable Kates at home whose tongues they are incapable of tying. Petruchio, as a walking, talking bridle and cucking-stool, will effect on the stage on behalf of the impotent audience and community the victory life seldom affords. Not only will Petruchio tame his shrew but she will come to adore and proclaim her tamed condition; or at any rate she will seem to do so.

The jaded conviction that every woman is a shrew at heart comforted the individual male in his affliction. Adam Eyre, a Yorkshireman, grumbled into his diary, 'This morn my wife began, after her old manner, to brawl and revile me for criticizing her clothing and stepping on her foot and she kept on till noon' (*Dyurnall*, June 1647, p. 46). Built into this morose statement of grievance is the sense that woman's scolding is inveterate and constitutional; stemmed for the time being, it will break out afresh 'after her old manner'. Assuming adverse criticism of a wife's personal appearance to be unexceptionable, and dismissing the possible provocation of stepping on someone's foot, Eyre is riled by the bilious longevity of the woman's nagging: 'and she kept on till noon'. The wife's clacking tongue is read as the insolent signal of her fundamental uncontrollability. And marriage, that haven to the male after the labours of the day, becomes a confinement with a mindless companion obsessed with sartorial vanity and minor or fancied injuries. Thus do the hens of patriarchy, bred for show and fed on ignorance, come home to roost. The scolded middle-class male might take comfort from the observation that even the most august households might be ruled, split asunder or given notoriety by a woman who refuses to know her place. The powerful Elizabeth, Countess of Shrewsbury (Bess of Hardwick), having amassed a fortune from previous marriages, carried on with business affairs and with building and restoration work at Chatsworth and Hardwick as if she were a 'feme sole'. Bishop Overton wrote to her estranged husband in 1590 in an attempt to initiate reconciliation:

But some will say . . . that the countess is a sharp and bitter shrew . . . Indeed, my good lord, I have heard some say so, but if shrewdness or sharpness may be a just cause of separation . . . I think few men in England would keep their wives long; for it is a common jest, yet true in some sense, that there is but one shrew in the world, and every man hath her.

(in Hogrefe, 1975, p. 70)

A 'shrew' in medieval and Renaissance usage could refer either to a man or a woman, and Shakespeare uses it thus in *The Shrew* when Curtis calls Petruchio 'more shrew than she' (IV.1.76), but usage tended towards the female. The adjective 'shrewd', used here misogynistically by the Bishop, had not yet fully acquired its modern meaning of 'astute' or 'acute'. It conveyed the supposed malignant characteristics of the rodent and, if used in connection with qualities of intellect, implied artfulness or cunning. Yet Bess, a shrew in the old sense, was also powerfully shrewd in the forthcoming one, not only in amassing a financial empire but in designing and building new houses according to the magnificent Italian Renaissance principles. Bishop Overton, who attempts to calm her irate husband by presenting the deviant Countess as a regrettable norm, refers her psychopathology back to female frailty: 'I doubt not but your great wisdom and experience hath taught you to bear some time with woman as the weaker vessel' (see Hogrefe, 1975, p. 70). The ambitious building projects of Bess, monuments to her own magnificence, represent the achievements of the shrew that got away: one in ten thousand. She could do this solely because she was propertied in her own right. The economic power she commanded licensed her almost uniquely both to act and to speak.

But the 'scold' is near cousin to the witch. Here Shakespeare's play lightly brushes against one of the deepest sources of male sexual terror. The tamer in this comedy wizards the potential witch away. He is a fantasy not only of male potency in the phallic swagger of his violent idiolect but also of power to rule his roost in such a manner as to pre-empt his own deepest fears. Hurling food and drink around his country house in Act IV, attacking his servants and persecuting the tailor, Petruchio plays out for the audience a fantasy of domestic domination, madly whacking and insulting his underlings while he steadily talks them and his wife down: 'Sit down, Kate, and welcome.

17

od, food, food!' (1.128). Petruchio is distinguished from the
...males not simply by his outrageous displays of aggression but
by the fact that he alone is not afraid of Kate. 'Tush, tush, fear
boys with bugs!' he boasts in the first act (2.208). The excess of horror
induced in the patriarchs and suitors of Padua by Kate's wildcat
disposition in relation to the actually quite limited extent of her violence,
is a comic reflection of the pathological fear which detected a witch in
every poor addled old widow, infernally beautiful woman or girl-
prodigy with apparently supra-normal powers. In the fifteenth to seventeenth centuries, Europe flamed with bonfires: villages and towns could
supply apparently infinite quantities of malignant and disaffected
females given to cursing their neighbours or chatting with their cats.
Beauty itself is commonly said to be 'bewitching', and the sexual act,
for which a man hazards all 'For the poor benefit of a bewitching
minute' (Tourneur/Middleton, *The Revenger's Tragedy*, III.5.75), implies a loss of control and autonomy in the male that he might fearfully
ascribe to the demonic affiliations of womankind. Colleague of the
serpent in Eden, Eve bred daughters who were susceptible to possession
and congress, both sexual and spiritual, with the devil and his incubi.
In 1600 most respectable people believed in the existence of witches, the
last execution of a witch in England taking place in Exeter in 1685. On
the Continent whole villages had been emptied of their female popula-
tions in the waves of mass hysteria that periodically devastated Europe.
Between 1587 and 1593 (around the date of *The Shrew*), twenty-two
villages around Trier surrendered 368 witches to the bonfires. In 1577,
the Toulouse region burned 400 (see O'Faolain and Martines, p. 215).
Fear of witches and legislation against them were ancient and primitive:
a thought-provoking law in the code of the sixth-century Franks states
that 'If a witch eats a man and it can be proven that she did this,' a fine
of 8,000 denarii is payable (see Amt, p. 43).

So witches *eat* men. The infantile fear of being eaten up for dinner by
the person you expect to feed you – the consumer consumed – is
replayed in the hysterical witch-hunts of the period. Male fear of the
swallowing of identity into a dominating mother-figure provokes orgies
of repression. Shakespeare's Kate of course is not a witch. But the
scold lived in the house next door to the witch. While the scold's furies
were a private and public nuisance, the witch's curses indicated a desire
and power to hurt individuals and to damage the community by
invoking the powers of darkness. The one could easily slide over into
the other, if the tongue's maledictions were attributed with capacity to
cause harm. Viewed in this light, the full extent of Kate's impotence

comes into focus. For, notwithstanding that Bianca's balked suitors consider the elder sister to be a 'fiend of hell' (I.1.88), this language never escapes the carnivalesque world of farce. Kate, who is handsome but not bewitching, is pinned into the class and commercial structure in a peculiarly deadly way. She rails and shouts, the play suggests, because of her powerlessness and not as an expression of power. Having no magic to call upon, she expresses sore and indignant feelings every time she opens her mouth. A psychology is implied for her, compounded of sibling rivalry for the father's affections, which are monopolized by the shrewd (but not yet shrewish) younger daughter, and wounded pride at the social disgrace of being a suitorless undesirable because she has fallen back on her only available weapon, aggression:

> Nay, now I see
> She is your treasure, she must have a husband.
> I must dance bare-foot on her wedding-day,
> And for your love to her lead apes in hell.
> Talk not to me, I will go sit and weep,
> Till I can find occasion of revenge.
>
> (II.1.31–6)

All Kate can do to express her mortification at being an object of public ridicule is to parade that mortification in the public arena so as to embarrass her father by making a parallel spectacle of him in front of the community from whose esteem his dignity derives. And she does obtain a series of small but sour-tasting gratifications in pursuing this policy: 'Was ever gentleman thus grieved as I?' Baptista laments after this tirade (37).

In a hierarchical society where marriage was woman's sole destiny, Kate's violence to Bianca in this scene, tying her up, striking and pursuing her with a view to further assault, expresses the uncontrollable panic of one who not only expects to end on the scrap heap but to do so in full view of a mocking community ('I must dance bare-foot on her wedding-day,' alluding to the custom by which an elder sister overtaken to the altar by a younger performed a festive ritual of humiliation – festive, that is, to all but herself). Kate's dedication to 'revenge' is not the maleficence of a witch with power to affect people and events but the burning resentment of the undervalued. Bianca's silence, interpreted as maidenly modesty by one and all (mistakenly, as the play reveals) is a far more powerful weapon than Kate's tongue. As Baptista's 'treasure', she is a material and emotional asset to her father: her silence is an economy, which hoards value without committing itself to expenditure. Kate recognizes Bianca's power and the aggression in her silence:

BAPTISTA   For shame, thou hilding of a devilish spirit,
             Why dost thou wrong her that did ne'er wrong thee?
             When did she cross thee with a bitter word?
KATHERINA Her silence flouts me, and I'll be revenged.

(II.1.26-9)

This line spoken in the theatre invariably brings the house down. But in its bloody-minded perversity lurks a signal truth: Bianca plays the system successfully, and the system is founded upon a competition among the females for the males. Kate fights the system, single-handedly, without focus or ally, and without hope of success. The system encompasses and controls her life rigorously, its hold on her destiny being only endorsed by her sister's collusion. Hence Bianca's silence 'flouts' Kate by drawing attention to her loud-mouthed and objectionable anomalousness. Bianca's silence speaks volumes and, as the comedy goes on to reveal, each volume is a pack of lies. The counterfeit meekness of a still tongue is a cover for a hidden willpower which, when her father is out of the way, expresses her resolute dedication to having what she wants and doing as she pleases. In Act III, Bianca advises the two 'tutors' to cease haggling for priority, since her education 'resteth in my choice', and she will 'learn my lessons as I please myself' (III,1,17; 20). The play voices the age's suspicion that all women are a law unto themselves, both those who apparently comply and those who chafe against constraints. 'It is better to dwell in the corner of the housetop, than with a brawling woman in a wide house,' remarks the Book of Proverbs feelingly (21:9), sparking a pleasing image of multitudinous husbands seeking attic sanctuary while the wives' tongues sound off below in the living-rooms. *The Taming of the Shrew* offers one brawling woman and an alternative, apparently demure, obedient, feminine. But once married, Bianca becomes proverbial. She answers back, won't come at her master's call, and gives as good as she gets. The play suggests that a man has two alternatives: a shrew . . . and a shrew.

2. 'Admitting My Life was Finished'

In 1991, the Chinese-American novelist Amy Tan published *The Kitchen God's Wife*, an account of two generations of mother and daughter, the first being born into the old Chinese traditions of forced marriage and intricate rites of subservience, the second into the liberal assumptions of modern America. Each woman, bonded so deeply to one another, is also a foreigner to the other. In hearing her mother's narrative of her life, the daughter learns deep truths of her own origins and identity. The mother breaks her silence to give her daughter access to the unsaid and almost unsayable. Her history is one of stoical endurance of humiliation and deprivation; but it also transmits a programme of resistance, which is understood not simply as testimony of an immemorial female subculture, but as the testament of the individual woman in the solitary confinement of a marriage that accords neither rights nor freedom. Though the mode of the novel is poignantly comic, a slow wave of sadness builds in the reader over the course of several hundred pages, with a power to draw tears from extraordinarily deep within the psyche. This is done by the simplest of telling:

[T]hat summer the cabbage was bad, the flavor of the bad water it drank. When Wen Fu asked me how I liked the dish, I was honest. 'Bitter,' I said. The next night he ordered the cook to make that same dish for me, nothing else.

He smiled and asked me again, 'Now, how do you like it?' I answered the same way as before. Night after night, it was the same question, the same answer, the same dish the next day. I had to eat that bitter cabbage or nothing. But I didn't give up. I waited for Wen Fu to grow tired of this cabbage game. And after two weeks' time, my stomach proved stronger than his temper.

Maybe this seems like a foolish thing, to be so stubborn over a bad-tasting cabbage. I could have lied and said, 'Tonight the food is delicious.' But if I didn't fight, wouldn't that be like admitting my life was finished?

(Amy Tan, *The Kitchen God's Wife*, p. 282)

The husband's attempt to control his wife through food, the basis of life and the mother's first gift to her child, implies the infantile basis of the male craving for dominance. Petruchio exhibits similar symptoms in *The Shrew*, whipping the food away from under Kate's very eyes, and even allowing his servant to bait her by proxy along the same lines: 'What say you to a neat's foot? . . . How say you to a fat tripe finely broiled? . . . What say you to a piece of beef and mustard?' (IV.3.17; 20; 23). There, of course, it is supposed to be a joke. In *The Kitchen God's Wife* it is no joke, though the focus of struggle is only that humble vegetable, cabbage. Wen Fu requires his wife's acquiescence in a form of words. As long as she withholds them, he will withhold sustaining food: those are the conditions of his 'game'. In one sense, she knows, her resistance must appear idiotic and self-spiting. For he exacts a trivial concession that is easily made and would cost her nothing but a few mouthfuls of air. And she need not mean what she says. However, since the wife has no power in practice or in law to resist the husband's tyranny, the refusal to speak the required formula is magnified into a private sign of immense significance. That speech-act becomes a life-and-death issue. She will tolerate rapes, public insult, infidelity and mockery because she has no choice, but she will not concede with her tongue that the cabbage which that same tongue knows to be nasty is really 'delicious'. Her sense that she still possesses a self, which she holds in esteem, abused and abased as it is, depends on her ability to hold true to the word 'bitter' as a description of a bitter thing, and to refuse to mouth the cowed and cynical lie that 'Tonight the food is delicious.' A kind of heroism is displayed here, together with a victory that, negligible in itself, symbolizes a defiant refusal to acknowledge that 'my life was finished'.

Wen Fu tires of his game. Petruchio does not tire of his, but pursues it through to the bitter end – which is presented to the audience by both wife and husband as a sweet end. Katherina is brought to declare the equivalent of 'Tonight the food is delicious.' This lie is the price she has finally decided to pay for the food she really wants, which is love, attention, a sense of value from her husband, together with a respected place in society. The nasty cabbage of male supremacy can under such circumstances be perceived by the palate as quite good, if swallowing it is the sole means to secure these ends. *The Shrew* advertises itself as a comedy, and we have bought a ticket for laughter. To make this easier for civilized viewers, Shakespeare has carefully excluded physical assault from Petruchio's programme of taming stunts, deflecting violence on to the persons of the servants (non-persons), whom Kate also beats at in her frustration. Petruchio abstains from striking her, though he threatens to when she hits out at him: 'I swear I'll cuff you, if you strike again' (II.1.218), and the point is made that he does not rape her, each of these being possible courses of action legitimately open to the husband of an incorrigible wife. On his wedding night, he is described by a servant as 'In her chamber,/Making a sermon of continency to her' (IV.1.168–9).

He rather shames her on the public stage and both stints and uproariously confounds her in the sanctum of the home, all in the name of devoted conjugal love. The wife in Amy Tan's novel is used and abused without mercy, as a thing owned. Although Petruchio claims his wife too as 'my goods, my chattels' (III.2.229), Shakespeare's genre slants towards romantic comedy, allowing for the possible growth of sexual attraction between the cavorting husband and the spirited wife, romanticizing the image of the wife-tamer and stylizing his improvisations into a stunning performance-art of sexual display, and ensuring that the hero does not cause his mate any actual bodily harm.

How then is it apt to draw a comparison between *The Kitchen God's Wife*, a tragicomic modern realistic novel written by a woman, and *The Taming of the Shrew*, a light-hearted Tudor comedy composed by a man, acted originally by men and boys, for the entertainment of a largely male audience? I would reply that China and England are one territory, ruled by variations on the same code of laws and social pressures; that the two texts are twins begotten by the one father. In *The Shrew*, Kate seems to emerge victorious; she appears happy and assured in her husband's love and admiration. 'If you can't beat them, join them,' has been the time-honoured counsel of the realist. In *The Kitchen God's Wife*, the unloved wife seems ground into the dust. Yet in her minuscule acts and speeches of resistance, she continues the fight which signifies to herself that her life is not finished; and this is not a battle conducted by indirection and subterfuge but through direct confrontation, a tactic that is abandoned by Shakespeare's Kate in the latter part of the play because she sees its futility. Kate's life is finished, because she concedes her voice. At the end of *The Taming of the Shrew*, Kate Minola is dead as the person she was. But the wife in Amy Tan has survived to tell her tale to her daughter.

Behind Shakespeare's play but camouflaged by it lie the shame of the cucking-stool and the horror of the brank. These implements of torture were traumatic to the victim, though they brought the whole community out of doors, in a spirit of festival, to parade around town hooting at the scold as she underwent her ritual humiliation. *The Shrew* ducks Kate in the tainted water of our mirth, as her sisters were immersed in the mire of the horse-pond. It parades her before us as the bridled scold was ridden round the market-place to universal taunts and jeers, to be tethered to some post and there spat and pissed upon by the populace. Let us consider the bridle. Only one account by a wearer is known to exist, that of a Quaker, Dorothy Waugh, printed in 1656. She describes how her vocal public Puritan resistance to the secular authority led to summary sentence by the Mayor of Carlisle. The instrument was:

[A] stone weight of Iron . . . & three barrs of Iron to come over my face, and a peece of it was put in my mouth, which was so unreasonable big a thing for that place as cannot be well related, which was locked to my head, and so I stood their time with my hands bound behind me with the stone weight of Iron upon my head and the bitt in my mouth to keep me from speaking; And the Mayor said he would make me an Example . . .

(in Boose, p. 206)

The fact that this personal account found its way into print at all is a testament to the power of Quakerism's doctrine of the 'inner light' for both men and women, with its emphasis on the close connection of the light of faith to the Light that created the world, of human language to the Word of God. No earthly bridle is heavy, cruel or mortifying enough to silence the spirit. A 'stone weight of Iron' was not enough to shame Dorothy Waugh into silence. On the contrary, it was a shameful sign of the persecution of the faithful by the ungodly – an article of the devil's manufacture. Dorothy was authorized and empowered by this violation to broadcast her truth in print. It is no accident that this sole-surviving piece of documentary evidence in a woman's hand stems from the interregnum period when – for a brief space – some women, belonging to the sects or 'gathered churches' and supported by the fellowship of other believers, found their voices. Prophetesses spoke in the market-place; women stood up in church and testified, conversion 'relations' or narratives spoken or read to the entire congregation being the entrance test to the separatist churches (see Caldwell, pp. 1–25). The best known of the women religious writers and speakers is Margaret Fell, whose treatise, *Women's Speaking Justified* (1667), rehabilitates women from St Paul's aspersions: 'Christ in the Male and the Female is one, where he hath poured forth his Spirit upon them, they must prophesie, though blind Priests say to the contrary and will not let holy women to speak' (see Fell, p. 13). The preacher, Katherine Chidley, voiced the same opinion in print as early as 1641: 'I know of no true Divinity that teacheth men to be Lords over the Conscience' (see Ezell, p. 109). But these developments took place half a century after Shakespeare's Katherina spoke up for herself against a background of threat. The iron headpiece, which was intended by the authorities as a parody crown, could be reinterpreted by a later generation as a crowning spiritual glory, symbol of freedom and union with Christ – the soul's true 'bridal'.

For the run of women, their solitude and anomalousness in the community would always militate against any such empowerment. Big-talkers and vehemently angry people do not always know why they cannot guard their tongues or keep their own counsel. The sources of their discontent may be bewilderingly opaque to them, and if asked why they nag their husbands and annoy their neighbours with eternal torrents of words they may not be able to invoke Eternal Truth or political principle. The brank would probably have a deterrent effect on anyone in her right mind. It was secured by padlock, so that the head was effectively caged. Its most terrifying feature was the piece of metal, varying from one and a half to three inches in length, which was fixed to the inner part of the iron hoop and forced into the mouth of the victim, pressing the tongue down. This would cause her to retch or vomit, especially if she panicked. The invasive piece of iron was either flat, or turned up or down, sometimes covered in prongs which caused the tender interior of the mouth to bleed. Often the bridle was painted in gay colours, the 'bitt' being red. At the back or side a chain was attached, with an iron ring at the end through which a rope could be threaded, to pull the victim along and to secure her to a post or hook. It is likely that every tug of the rope would draw blood, break teeth and even shatter the jaw-bone of the victim.

So Kate got off very lightly. If Petruchio is not himself a living version of the scold's bridle – a brightly coloured, ingenious source of peremptory control – he represents a romantically palatable alternative to the bridle. The contemporary audience knew this. When, at the culmination of his soliloquy in Act IV in which he explains his methods to the audience, he throws out the challenge:

> And thus I'll curb her mad and headstrong humour.
> He that knows better how to tame a shrew,
> Now let him speak – 'tis charity to show.
>
> (1.195–7)

the word 'curb' picks up the submerged image of a horse's bridle, and 'headstrong', implying rashness and wilfulness, reinforces it by the suggestion of a horse wildly thrusting against the curb to get its head. Society's curb for scolds was a punitive piece of engineering which forcibly dissuaded her from speaking her mind; the husband was furnished with a natural curb. And the resort to law to control a rampant-tongued woman was stigmatized as a failure of the phallus. The scold's bridle forces its way into the mouth as the husband's phallus enters the wife in that second mouth, the vagina. The analogy

25

between the two orifices was proverbial. In his Elegie XVIII, 'Loves Progress', Donne explained that:

> Rich Nature hath in women wisely made
> Two purses, and their mouths aversely laid:
>
> (91–2)

In *A Shrew* the sexual implications of the curb image are clearer, for in the soliloquy of Ferando that corresponds to Petruchio's, the hawk image is subordinated to that of the horse to be broken:

> This humor must I holde me to a while,
> To bridle and hold backe my headstrong wife,
> With curbes of hunger: ease: and want of sleepe,
> Nor sleepe nor meate shall she injoie to night.
> I'll mew her up as men do mew their hawkes,
> And make her gently come unto the lure,
> Were she as stuborne or as full of strength
> As were the *Thracian* horse *Alcides* tamde,
> That King *Egeus* fed with flesh of men,
> Yet would I pull her downe and make her come
> As hungry hawkes do flie unto there lure.
>
> (*A Shrew*, p. 68)

A Shrew's editors (see Holderness and Loughrey, p. 26) emphasize the sexuality of the bridling imagery in Ferando's speech. The 'curbes of hunger' Ferando will put into operation will act to arouse her appetite not for pork or beef but for 'flesh of men'. Ravenous Kate will be subdued to her 'natural' female desire to take man's flesh into her body. Hence 'pull[ing] her downe and mak[ing] her come' becomes not the bridling but the satisfaction of the natural urges she had denied. Later, Ferando arrives with 'a peece of meate uppon his daggers point' (p. 70), but Kate rejects the offered food, refusing to 'be beholding to you for your Meate' (p. 71). The phallic implications of the feeding imagery could hardly be called subtle.

This equation of the social necessity for women to be mastered with women's sexual desire to be overpowered ('ridden') by men opens the way to the 'sexy' interpretation of *The Shrew*, according to which Kate's rejection of Petruchio's brazen advances is interpreted as a great unconscious come-on. The explosive violence between them is seen as eroticism, the power-relationship a manifestation of sexual excitement. Burton and Taylor, and O'Toole and Peggy Ashcroft exemplified in their different ways such an approach to the play, in which the shrew is seen as rescued from her sterile situation and provoked into vivid life, which converts her aggression into sexual energy (see pp. 48–9 below).

Petruchio absorbs her in a game which guarantees her, if not comfort, at least a version of the intense attention she had needed and lacked. The play thus becomes a rough-and-tumble rescue operation whose destination is the bed to which the 'couple of quiet ones' disappear at the end of the play: 'Come, Kate, we'll to bed' (V.2.183) – and *Exeunt*, eagerly. Under this interpretation, Kate has not lost her self but found it. She is (although she doesn't know it until the last act) happiest with his tongue in her mouth.

The message of the play seems to be twofold. Not only do men desire to tame women (a process which both arouses and gratifies their sexual desire, especially if the woman does not give in easily) but women desire to be mastered. That is their underlying nature, which is reached by making them lie under a man and take his whole weight, until they give up struggling. The process involves making not only a fool but a horse of the woman, who must be saddled, bridled, mounted, ridden and made to perform according to the commands of the owner, for she is 'My horse, my ox, my ass, my any thing' (III.2.231). As the hawk is brought down from her high station, so the bucking mare is gripped between the legs of her master and ridden half to death. The sexuality implicit in this symbolism is of ancient vintage and pornographic provenance, which is lightly touched on in *The Shrew*. Equestrianism was synonymous in the period with caste: the Lord and his hunters ride the high horse of rank and authority, the heraldry which blazons aristocratic privilege having its origins in a horse culture, based on horsepower (hence the word 'chivalry', from the French *cheval*, 'horse', and *chevalerie*, 'knighthood'). In the first act, Petruchio in a swaggering speech makes it clear that he is not one to be daunted by a woman's tongue, being a man of the world – a man's world of exotic adventure, sea voyages, the field of war:

> Think you a little din can daunt mine ears?
> Have I not in my time heard lions roar?
> Have I not heard the sea, puffed up with winds,
> Rage like an angry boar chafèd with sweat?
> Have I not heard great ordnance in the field,
> And heaven's artillery thunder in the skies?
> Have I not in a pitchèd battle heard
> Loud 'larums, neighing steeds, and trumpets' clang?
> And do you tell me of a woman's tongue,
> That gives not half so great a blow to hear
> As will a chestnut in a farmer's fire?
> Tush, tush, fear boys with bugs!
>
> (I.2.197–208)

27

Thus the tinpot Othello declares his male credentials in a punchy and bellicose array of rhetorical questions, designed to make the nervous manhood of Padua, and especially perhaps the querulous pantaloon Gremio, gape. He has bestridden, he gives them to understand, the world; adventured the elements and been among the cavalry (again, from the Norman, *chevalerie*, and Italian *cavalleria*) on the heroic field of war. The energy and excitement of the speech, with its resounding comparisons (the crashing sea like a raging boar in a hunt, the cannonade of the storm and the inferno of battle) put the little men of Padua in their places. He is a potent male; they are puny lads. Kate in this rhetorical dimension pops like 'a chestnut in a farmer's fire'. The stay-at-home Paduans are rather impressed.

The sheer machismo of Petruchio's speeches has a spectacular quality which stands out equally against the prosaic speech-patterns of the natives and the romantic loquacity of the city's other visitor, Lucentio. The Paduans grumble, scheme, quarrel and neurotically count their money. Petruchio rides language like a kicking horse, showing off all the acrobatic skills of his horsemanship, relishing his dominance of language and his 'rope-tricks' (I.2.110). Thrust and vigour characterize his speech, advertising virility in a gymnastic discourse of juggling and tumbling as he spars with Kate in their first prolonged wit-bout (II.1.182–271); outrageous displays of extempore reversal (II.1.283–310, his proclamation of Kate's love in the teeth of her denial) and the manic drive of his imagination in which he feigns a chivalrous rescue of his bride from the non-existent onslaught of the reeling wedding guests:

> Touch her whoever dare!
> I'll bring mine action on the proudest he
> That stops my way in Padua. Grumio,
> Draw forth thy weapon, we are beset with thieves,
> Rescue thy mistress if thou be a man.
> Fear not, sweet wench, they shall not touch thee, Kate.
> I'll buckler thee against a million.

(III.2.232–8)

It is as if Shakespeare had imported that stallion Harry Hotspur from his history play into the peacetime world of comedy, giving the hot-blooded young man nothing to do but the comic business of wife-hunting. Petruchio exercises wit and muscle in an arena where he is compassed about by flaccid specimens. His antics and their consummation present to the men of Padua and those in the audience a sign of spectacular genital endowment. As for Kate, she is first invited to ride ('sit on me' (II.1.198)) at their initial meeting and then to 'bear' the

28

burden of his weight, as a horse or ass does its rider (199–205), to which she retaliates by saying that she will bear 'No such jade as you', a jade being a clapped-out horse. Such a 'jade' will be described in the third act, a scrofulous nag on which the groom-like bridegroom is described as riding to his marriage. Petruchio and his horse seem to make up a partnership that focuses both his relationship to his servants and to his wife. Act IV opens with Grumio trudging on, bemoaning his beaten, muddied, cold and exhausted state after his cross-country journey with his mad master: 'Fie, fie on all tired jades, on all mad masters, and all foul ways!' (1.1–2). He gives his subordinate servant, Curtis, a knockabout version of a striking tale, accompanied by a cuff on the ear in the manner of his master. The tale concerns a master, a mistress, a horse and a servant:

GRUMIO First know my horse is tired, my master and mistress fallen
        out.
CURTIS How?
GRUMIO Out of their saddles into the dirt, and thereby hangs a tale.

                                                                (47–51)

This off-stage horseplay has an edge of sexual innuendo, which is pointed up by Grumio's feigning to take offence when Curtis asks if the husband and wife were on one horse: 'What's that to thee?' (62). Then he proceeds to explain how, for his impertinence, Curtis will not be told the tale of

[H]ow her horse fell, and she under her horse; thou shouldst have heard in how miry a place, how she was bemoiled, how he left her with the horse upon her, how he beat me because her horse stumbled, how she waded through the dirt to pluck him off me, how he swore, how she prayed that never prayed before, how I cried, how the horses ran away, how her bridle was burst, how I lost my crupper – with many things of worthy memory, which now shall die in oblivion, and thou return unexperienced to thy grave.

                                                                (65–75)

These things are a parable. The bridleless bride is dunked in the mud. The out-of-hand horse rolls upon her and her groom leaves her in the mire: a mire, it is suggested, of her own choosing. When the woman puts on breeches, the horse rides the man. The appropriate punishment is for the horse to ride the woman. The swamp into which Grumio's account up-ends Kate combines elements of the scold's freezing dip in the horse-pond on the cucking-stool with the mortifying bridle that curbs her like a horse. Because these events are narrated rather than shown, they are a distanced form of farce, further deflected by the point of the joke, which is not the events in themselves but the heroic consequence Grumio ascribes to these horsings-about which, in refusing to tell, he details exactly. Little of this equine business is present in *A Shrew*, but so much is made of it in Shakespeare's fourth act that the unseen steed features in the action alongside the other 'jades' as an aspect of Petruchio and his menage. His remorseless high spirits as he overrides his wife's resistance are conveyed in the very rhythms of his speaking voice, with its casual but restless colloquialisms ('With ruffs and cuffs and farthingales and things' (IV.3.56); 'Here's snip and nip and cut and slish and slash' (90); 'Nothing but sit and sit, and eat and eat!' (V.2.12)). This big-talker would rather be doing than speaking; riding hard than sitting still.

The way we feel about and for Kate as the recipient of this violent assault of words and action is rendered complex and problematic not only by the reaction we bring to the ideology of the play but also by the methods by which Shakespeare characterizes Kate and the quality of that characterization. Is she presented as an individual personality, a figure of farce or a stereotype shrew? My own feeling is that she is an example of incomplete characterization which has been limited and rendered unstable by the misogynist ideology to which the shrew belongs and the popular farce that is its native mode. In other words, Kate is a hybrid, compounded of incompatible elements, squeezed into an untenable space at the juncture between genres. Neither a pantomime horse nor a fully represented individual, her back end is horse, her front portions woman. Lawrence Sterne in *Tristram Shandy* had Tristram's father explode with indignation at Uncle Toby:

Methinks, brother . . . you might, at least, know so much as the right end of a woman from the wrong.

. . . Right end, quoth my uncle Toby . . . Right end of a woman!—I declare, quoth my uncle, I know no more which it is, than the man in the moon;—and if I was to think, continued my uncle Toby, (keeping his eyes still fixed upon the bad joint) this month together, I am sure I should not be able to find it out.

(*Tristram Shandy*, Volume II, chapter 7)

Uncle Toby's vestal innocence is an unusual variation on a confusion endemic to less virginal male culture: the double bind that views the lower parts of woman as animal, the higher features as human, and tries to make sense of its bastardizing vision and muddled emotions. In tragic terms we see this complex emerging from *King Lear*'s subconscious mind as it focuses womanhood (in the persons of Goneril and Regan) as dual:

> Down from the waist they are centaurs,
> Though women all above;
> But to the girdle do the gods inherit,
> Beneath is all the fiends' –
> (*King Lear*, IV.6.124–7)

Female animality below the waist is irreconcilable with the womanliness of the person above it. Genital heat (of lust and venereal disease) rages like a mare in oestrus and threatens like hellfire, while the face and breast reflect the promise of heaven. Lear's fantasy focuses the male terror of female sexual power.

The Shrew's plot affirms the identity of the 'right end' and the 'wrong end' in a fantasy of male sexual control. But the play undermines its own ideology by presenting the rudiments of personality in Katherina in a naturalistic bourgeois realism which contradicts the dynamic thrust of the plot dominated by Petruchio, with its roots in popular farce and folk-tale. His bounding sexual energy and the patriarchal programme of reconstruction it authorizes are in conflict with the tendency of this realism to humanize Katherina and create sympathy for her plight and problems. But that conflict is unequal. The characterization of Kate never develops far enough to present a significant challenge to the fast-moving ebullience of her tamer's activities. Yet its presence disturbs and arrests us by hints of who Kate is and how she came to be that person. The taming of a shrew is also an assault on a person, one in a weak and vulnerable position with an implied history of neglect behind her. She is also a singularly ordinary girl, whose speech is lowbrow, plain, undignified and homely. Indeed, she seems at first almost inarticulate. The burghers and artisans who have come to watch the play may have left just such a daughter flouncing round the house; their pleasure at the sight of Mr Minola's embarrassed inability to cope with his stroppy, graceless child would therefore be spiced with *Schadenfreude*.

Surely the most extraordinary paradox in this problematic play is how little of a shrew Kate actually appears to be. She seems at first sullen and miserable rather than actively cantankerous. We see and hear her very little in the first act, though the complaints of her rowdiness are deafening. Producers eke this out by having her stamp and flail around the stage. The initial sketch of Kate in Act I, scene 1 is brief, and suggestive rather than searching, but if we explore its implications in detail the result may point up the extent to which a minimal but persuasive case history and psychology are implied for Kate, arousing sympathy the more one reflects. However, the play does not allow us to pause for reflection. It whirls the audience on through farce,

31

knockabout and the virtuoso eloquence of Petruchio, whose unstoppable energy stampedes all such considerations. The first scene in which the Minola family appears would surely be a gift to the transactional analyst or to students of family therapy. Kate is first viewed in a family context, flanked by her father and sister, between whom a complicit understanding exists. They stroke one another in the public arena with socially proper words of blandishment. Baptista counts on being obeyed by the younger daughter, who gains in worth in direct ratio to the unbiddable Kate's sulks, sneers and retorts:

BAPTISTA   Bianca, get you in.
                And let it not displease thee, good Bianca,
                For I will love thee ne'er the less, my girl.
KATHERINA A pretty peat! It is best
                Put finger in the eye, an she knew why.
BIANCA   Sister, content you in my discontent.
                Sir, to your pleasure humbly I subscribe.
                My books and instruments shall be my company,
                On them to look and practise by myself.

(I.1.75–83)

A familiar model of family dynamics is here set out before us. The father, who cannot deal with the envy of the unlovable elder daughter, turns in relief to the acceptable younger, whom he addresses with tenderness, though not without anxiety, since in refusing to let her marry before her sister he is thwarting her natural ambitions. He reminds her of her role as 'good Bianca', and his instruction to withdraw is made in the form of a near plea, with a statement of the reward attached to docility (love). The obedience of offspring reinforces paternal authority, which is ultimately dependent on their co-operation. In reinforcing the bond between himself and Bianca, he reminds the smarting elder daughter of her chronic sense of rejection. His warmth to Bianca repeats the original injury done to Kate (or perceived by herself as having been done) when the younger sibling was born and usurped parental affection; generating Kate's disaffection and turning her into a shrew. Hence, stung by yet another repetition of the original betrayal, she retorts in language as spiteful as it is infantile, against the younger sister, her father's 'peat' (pet), implying that Bianca is a manipulator who can turn on the attention-cadging tears at the least opportunity. The childishness of her speech-patterns, linguistic residue of the unresolved conflicts of childhood, does not invalidate her perception of Bianca's character. This turns out to be quite accurate, but is scarcely calculated to endear Katherina to anyone on the stage. The unprovoked attack plays straight into Bianca's hands, enabling her to show womanly qualities of martyred righteousness while covertly retaliating against her sister ('Sister, content you in my discontent'). She hands her father the carrot of the word 'humbly' and is able to represent herself as dedicated to solitary study, deferring to the authoritarian values of the civilized hierarchy that ordains woman's place and has decreed that she shall not marry until her sister has been sold off.

Kate says nothing. The so-called 'shrew' is out-talked, and for want of ammunition retires into dudgeon. She only breaks forth again when Bianca has left the stage, followed by her father who expressly forbids Kate to intrude upon the *tête-à-tête* he proposes with Bianca off-stage.

BAPTISTA   And so farewell. Katherina, you may stay,
           For I have more to commune with Bianca.
KATHERINA Why, and I trust I may go too, may I not?
           What, shall I be appointed hours, as though, belike,
           I knew not what to take and what to leave? Ha?

                                                      (100–104)

Kate is established as the odd one out, excluded from the intimacy enjoyed by her sister and the father who has exposed her to ridicule by offering her around to the available Paduan suitors, thus giving them the chance to reinforce his rejection with their own. The tensions and antagonisms within the family are presented both through the said and the not-said. For instance, Baptista rarely speaks directly to Kate if he can help it, and presumably avoids eye contact. Her exclamations of protest against being made 'a stale . . . amongst these mates' (58) are simply ignored by her father, who finally leaves her alone on the stage with Bianca's inflamed suitors, who have insulted and railed at her as a 'fiend of hell' (88) because her existence has balked them of their prize. Fulminating at the way her father's prohibition slights her dignity, she stomps after him, to make an unwelcome third at his private discussion with Bianca. Her mode of departure succeeds in making her yet more undignified. Kate is seen as trapped in an emotional circle. Nobody wants her; she makes herself all the more objectionable so as to retaliate and solicit attention; in so doing, she reinforces their dislike and her own outsiderliness. Yet all this occurs in no more than fifty-five lines of the 500-odd of the first act, and Kate has only spoken twelve of those lines. The analysis for which I have had space here, and which is surely central to a play in which Kate counts as heroine,

33

remains in *The Shrew* at the stage of the embryonic and rudimentary. The centre is displaced to a point near the periphery: Kate is more often the object discussed than the active agent. And indeed, until the final soliloquy, it is not Kate but Petruchio who is the dramatic centre. The title says it all: *The Taming of the Shrew*: the comedy concerns not what the shrew does or is, but what is done to her and her reactions.

In the second act, the mode changes to active violence. Realism shifts into farce as Kate assaults her sister, smashes a lute over the tutor's head, engages with Petruchio and strikes him in the wit-bout, only to be devastated at her summary appropriation by the outrageous new-comer. In the first scene, Kate is discovered viciously tying Bianca's hands, interrogating her about her suitors, slapping her and finally rushing her in an apparent attempt at a flying tackle. If this is farce it is also observable that the interiors of many middle-class houses contain-ing adolescent daughters present daily scenes of the equivalent of such mayhem. Realism still prevails, provoking the reflection that what we are disposed to call farce may often be an unpalatable truth-to-life. Bianca, faced with her vengeful sister in full cry, cringes, and concedes everything she can think of that might be a source of envy, from rich clothes to suitors. However, as she doesn't care for her suitors, and there is doubtless plenty more finery where this came from (her doting father's pocket), this may not be much of a concession. What Kate really wants, as they both know, cannot be extracted from her sibling. This recognition is condensed into the immortal line, killingly funny when delivered in the theatre and deadly earnest when pondered at one's leisure: 'Her silence flouts me, and I'll be revenged' (II.1.29). Female silence is empty neither of meaning nor power: it is an open sign which can mock a loud-mouthed sister, hook a loquacious suitor and devise its own subversive gratification. Miming submission, it can function as a cast-iron means of dominance. Baptista apparently has to grapple hand-to-hand in an unseemly wrestle with his frenetic elder daughter ('What, in my sight? Bianca, get thee in' (30)) as Kate dives at her enemy, compulsively airing her causes of grievance when defeated of prey:

> What, will you not suffer me? Nay, now I see
> She is your treasure, she must have a husband.
> I must dance bare-foot on her wedding-day,
> And for your love to her lead apes in hell.
> Talk not to me, I will go sit and weep,
> Till I can find occasion of revenge.

> (31–6)

This well-observed sketch of tantrum and sibling rivalry spits out gall in the repeated stressed 'she' and conjures up a fantasy of what is most feared (public humiliation) with which to berate the parent. Beneath the rage is an unheard plea for denied love and restitution, which however the sufferer knows she is alienating yet further; hence, she terminates her tantrum in the self-therapy of threat. The audience laughs at the whirling stage activity, at the ineffectual paterfamilias, at the antics of Kate.

The rampant scene is cunningly placed to provide a comic foil for Petruchio to enter with all due and meet gravity, to put in an eloquent bid for the hand of this model of womanly virtue, famed for 'affability and bashful modesty,/. . . wondrous qualities and mild behaviour' (49–50), in a verse full of ironic symmetries and balance. Kate is off-stage for about 150 lines while Petruchio presents his violent and exotic credentials and bargains over the marriage contract. He heats up the audience's appetite for the contest of wills, mythologizing this conflict as the collision of 'two raging fires' (132), and presenting himself as a force of nature capable of extinguishing any blaze it encounters (135). Kate meanwhile is transferred from the stage to a narrative passage (the first of three: II.1.148–59; III.2.30–83; IV.1.64–75), where she is described as smashing the lute over the head of the supposed music teacher. The pillorying of the tutor, who is often presented reeling in wearing the instrument round his neck with an unstrung look upon his face, shifts the action away from the psychological to the pantomimic. The narrative mode includes snatches of direct and indirect speech ('"Frets, call you these? . . . I'll fume with them" . . . rascal fiddler/. . . twangling Jack' (II.1.152; 157–8)) which are vintage Kate, and which also shade into the folkloric. The events described are at once distanced and restaged in the theatre of audience fantasy. In the wit-bout, Petruchio has the first word and the last:

> Thou must be married to no man but me.
> For I am he am born to tame you, Kate,
> And bring you from a wild Kate to a Kate
> Conformable as other household Kates.
> (268–71)

From now on, Petruchio's appropriation of Kate's name and his systematic reversal of everything she has to say for herself become the focus of dramatic interest. His courtship has been described as 'nothing less than psychological rape – as the predominance of sexual puns in the scene emphasizes' (see Huston, p. 60). Yet the same critic goes on to explain that this 'psychological rape' is justified as part of a programme to impart to the stranded girl 'Petruchio's love of play and essential *joie de vivre*' (see Huston, p. 68), releasing her from her childhood trauma into a share in that intoxicating drama in which he takes the role of principal actor, playwright and director. 'In short,' says Huston, 'what Petruchio teaches Kate is his version of a lesson of modern psychoanalysis: man feels "only human when he plays"' (see Huston, p. 68).

The patriarchal bias of such a position is declared in the facile dalliance with the word 'rape', which is a functional counter for the critic, without connotations of real horror. The idea that rape, whether mental or physical, can be justified in a good cause, is outrageous; and no doubt if we pinned down the critic and demanded to know what he meant by this levity, he would squirmingly admit that he didn't really mean it: of course, as the play is a comedy, the 'rape' would occur only in 'play'. The idea of Petruchio as a kind of bouncing psychotherapist whose wild and vicious japes integrate his victim into a play-world of the two against all comers would be self-evidently bizarre in a world where people were *not* called upon routinely to believe that the sun is the moon (IV.5.1–16). But patriarchy has always required our assent to a code of delusions and *non sequiturs* based on the 'black-is-white' principle. For instance, when a woman says 'no' to sex, she is commonly held by the *cognoscenti* to mean 'yes' (because it is well known that women are naturally perverse). *The Shrew* enacts and authorizes a comic and therefore supposedly harmless variant on this evil. When Petruchio states that 'upon Sunday is the wedding-day', and Kate replies uncompromisingly, 'I'll see thee hanged on Sunday first' (II.1.291–2), Petruchio goes on to notify the community that, by mutual covenant, Kate's 'no' will always be a private code for 'yes':

> 'Tis bargained 'twixt us twain, being alone,
> That she shall still be curst in company.
>
> (297–8)

From this time on, Kate is effectively being bridled. She has, 'yes', been raped in the mouth, because her last resort, the capacity to resist with an angry 'no', which will register in the communal ear, is in process of elimination. During the wit-bout, Shakespeare has turned her back end to Petruchio and, with the obscene innuendo of the 'my tongue in your tail' jest, invited the audience to enjoy by proxy the view from the rear; to ride the mare in the saddle with the tamer.

The next two acts see her fitted with the bit and bridle, against which she rears in mounting panic and rage – panic and rage that are discountenanced moment by moment by our own laughter. That

36

laughter is complicit and reactionary. It is extorted by a Petruchio who is not just comic but a comedian, with a fresh gag and a novelty always up his sleeve – and, behind the game, a fist. He masters us as he dominates both Kate and Padua. Laughter is raised by Shakespeare through Petruchio every time he rapes Kate's mouth of the words and meaning she would utter. And to say that this is only in 'play', and that 'play' is an important thing that makes us 'only human' (see p. 36 above) is to abdicate the grounds of the human and humane, if those words mean anything at all. We have all watched children playing, and have played games ourselves. Though many traditional games reinforce stereotypical gender division – mothers and fathers, doctors and nurses – and hence prepare the child for socialization, it is observable that girls' most fulfilling games are girl-scripted, girl-centred and girl-directed. They are fantasies of mastery as positively as those of boys. But Shakespeare's Kate must have her dreams of power and autonomy snatched from her mouth. For *The Shrew* is a boys' game. The psychologists and psychoanalysts give the game away when they beget or foster such statements as Huston's to the effect that 'man' feels 'only human when he plays'. Our word for the species, being masculine ('man'), inevitably generates a masculine pronoun ('he'), covering a world of unexamined assumptions based on the confusion of humanity with the male. For what is 'she' doing and how is 'she' feeling when 'he' is enjoying 'his' game?

The abusive psychotherapy practised by Petruchio takes a considerable time to work on his impatient patient. Having promised to 'love, honour and obey' the sot who has claimed her as his wife at the altar he profanes, she breaks out in mutiny when he announces that they will not be staying for the wedding feast. She has come so far down from her high horse as to 'entreat' him to stay (III.2.198), and followed this up with unprecedented loving persuasion: 'Now if you love me stay' (203). Impudently pretending she has not spoken, Petruchio calls for his horse, to which his unfunnily berserk employee replies that 'the oats have eaten the horses' and Kate bursts forth in grievance:

> Nay then,
> Do what thou canst, I will not go today,
> No, nor tomorrow – not till I please myself.
> The door is open, sir, there lies your way,
> You may be jogging whiles your boots are green.
> For me, I'll not be gone till I please myself.
> 'Tis like you'll prove a jolly surly groom
> That take it on you at the first so roundly.

PETRUCHIO   O Kate, content thee, prithee be not angry.
KATHERINA   I will be angry – what hast thou to do?
                     Father, be quiet – he shall stay my leisure.
GREMIO   Ay marry, sir, now it begins to work.
KATHERINA   Gentlemen, forward to the bridal dinner.
                     I see a woman may be made a fool
                     If she had not a spirit to resist.
PETRUCHIO   They shall go forward, Kate, at thy command.
                     Obey the bride . . .

                                                                                      (206–22)

Taking the bit between her teeth, the bridled bride drags at her tether with a determined 'Nay then . . .' and, gathering courage and impetus, defies her husband's irrational command with an assertion of her own will. Her double insistence that she won't leave 'till I please myself' (208; 211) recalls Bianca's smooth but covert insistence on learning her lessons 'as I please myself' (III.1.20). The organization of this scene creates an ironic tension and suspense, as Petruchio gives his wife her head. First he pours out false unction (214), so that Kate gathers confidence, shutting up her father as if he were a child, and asserting matrimonial authority over her newly acquired spouse. The oats appear to be eating the horse. Gremio's taunt mocks Petruchio with having bitten off more than he can chew. Egged on thus, Kate flaunts her control, congratulating herself on her triumph and ceremoniously commanding the company ('Gentlemen, forward . . .') from her supposed position of power. Petruchio's apparent endorsement ('Obey the bride . . .') in fact mockingly commandeers her act of assertion as he sweeps her off the scene into the horrors of the honeymoon in Act IV.

Few apologists can be found for the tortures inflicted upon the solitary Katherina in Petruchio's country house: those who don't admit that their stomachs are turned confess to a touch of nervous dyspepsia at the Bard's brutalities. Here she is systematically deprived of food, warmth, sleep, attire, bearings, choice and language. In the first scene, Kate is stunned and very quiet. Next time she appears, she is baited by Grumio and retaliates, but then sits inert and listless, reduced to weary monosyllables expressive of a hopeless state of mind: 'Faith, as cold as can be' (IV.3.37). Her final major outburst comes in the haberdasher scene, in reaction to Petruchio's explanation (as of parent to child) of his behavioural principle of house-training. To her insistence that 'gentlewomen wear such caps as these', he replies, 'When you are gentle, you shall have one too,/And not till then'

(70–72). The matter of the cap (which recurs in the climax of th
is more important than modern dress codes equip us to rec
for the cap, worn indoors and out, would represent Kate's status
as a married woman. It was a double sign: of subordination and of
privilege, since the married woman (though deprived of rights in law)
enjoyed higher caste than the single. Petruchio will not allow Kate
this dignity without an absolute concession of his absolute rights. This
is unbearable:

KATHERINA Why, sir, I trust I may have leave to speak,
　　　　　And speak I will. I am no child, no babe.
　　　　　Your betters have endured me say my mind,
　　　　　And if you cannot, best you stop your ears.
　　　　　My tongue will tell the anger of my heart,
　　　　　Or else my heart concealing it will break,
　　　　　And rather than it shall, I will be free
　　　　　Even to the uttermost, as I please, in words.
PETRUCHIO Why, thou say'st true – it is a paltry cap

　　　　　　　　　　　　　　　　　　　　　　　(73–81)

In depriving Kate of a voice, Petruchio is implicitly returning her to
infancy; which (she says) she will absolutely not tolerate. She has a
voice. She intends to carry on using it. As a defence of a grown
person's right to express her mind, the speech is not without a certain
dignity, impelled by a strong thrust of indignation. However, in reminding her husband of her past-mastery of the ears of Padua (belonging to
those to whom she undiplomatically refers as 'your betters'), she no
doubt whets his appetite for the display of his virile taming qualifica-
tions. The relationship between 'tongue' and 'heart' draws our attention
to the burden of repression borne within by Kate in common with
every silenced woman: the pain of anger that swells uncontrollably the
longer it is denied. The relationship between unacknowledged anger
and personal breakdown, and the self-therapy of language, which
exorcizes what it expresses, is a recognition conventional in modern
psychology. Kate's speech is a straightforward and uncompromising
statement of individual freedom of will: 'I may . . . I will . . . I am . . .
will tell . . . will break . . . I will . . . I please.'

Petruchio simply disclaims her speech. He has not heard it. It has not
occurred. He carries on with his monkey-jabber. This is his way of
screwing the bridle down tighter on Kate's head and giving the reins
another hurtful yank, while smiling genially all over his face. But he
drops his act to give Kate a straightforward reprimand at the end of the

scene when she (rather politely, all things considered ('sir')) takes issue with his time-telling. By his clock it is seven in the morning; by hers (and reason's) two in the afternoon.

KATHERINA   I dare assure you, sir, 'tis almost two,
          And 'twill be supper-time ere you come there.
PETRUCHIO   It shall be seven ere I go to horse.
          Look what I speak, or do, or think to do,
          You are still crossing it. Sirs, let't alone,
          I will not go today, and ere I do,
          It shall be what o'clock I say it is.
HORTENSIO   Why, so this gallant will command the sun.

(IV.3.185–92)

This laying down of the law, in contradiction to natural law and the law of reason, is a perfect description of the disorder that underlies patriarchy. 'Sun', as Petruchio indicates two scenes later, is a pun for 'son'; and, as he is his 'mother's son' (IV.5.6), and as what the sons of the tribe say goes, the sun is the moon – if and when the son says so, and for as long as he chooses to maintain this opinion as ortho-dox. Language itself is an arbitrary sign-system fabricated and author-ized by patriarchy. Prompted by Hortensio, who points out that if Kate does not concur in the form of words dictated by her owner they will never set out for her father's house and their dinner, Kate capitulates:

PETRUCHIO   I say it is the moon.
KATHERINA   I know it is the moon.
PETRUCHIO   Nay, then you lie. It is the blessèd sun.
KATHERINA   Then, God be blessed, it is the blessèd sun.
          But sun it is not, when you say it is not,
          And the moon changes even as your mind.
          What you will have it named, even that it is,
          And so it shall be so for Katherine.

(5.16–22)

Weary irony is built into her agreement to 'Say as he says' (11). Since the moon is the proverbial emblem for the female principle, the 'blessed son's' inferior, fickle and changeable, and as *luna* was associated with lunacy and lunatics, Kate condemns her spouse as a moonstruck maniac even as she agrees to abide by his ever-changing nonsense-language. She implicitly hangs the motto *varium et mutabile semper* around his neck, which is as good as calling him a woman. Petruchio tests out the strength of her decision to abide by his irrational law by requiring her to greet the aged patriarch Vincentio as a gentlewoman, whose feminine charms he rapturously affirms. Kate acts her part, without apparent hesitation: 'Young budding virgin, fair and fresh and sweet,' she apostrophizes him/her (37), inquiring where he/she belongs and congratulating the destined husband of such a beauty on his prize. When Petruchio changes his mind and turns the maiden back into a male, Kate produces another virtuoso speech explaining that the sun got in her eyes. The son is permanently in her eyes from this point on. These speeches, with their exuberant and self-delighting poeticism, are often praised by critics as showing that, far from being squashed, Kate has simply learned to play her husband's supposedly liberating game, to display her spirit imaginatively, and to speak his joyous, festive language: 'In her response to Vincentio, Kate seems to have so fully approached Petruchio's vision that she talks like him' (see Huston, p. 90). I should rather think she had given up the ghost. Shakespeare has killed Kate off. For Kate was only ever words on a page. Her being was textual. She was not allowed many words to speak, but what she did say was her own, in a discourse of resistance we could recognize. But now, for all public purposes, she has *become* Petruchio. Petruchio I and Petruchio II share the centre-stage between them, speaking the same language and sealing their compact in the famous kiss (V.1.131–9). When Kate is summoned in to deliver her 'great' – I should rather say 'long' – harangue in Act V, she has become nothing but a walking incarnation of Petruchio's great Tongue. That monstrous Tongue in the guise of a woman is licensed for forty-four lines to maintain its supremacy at the centre of attention: 'Fie, fie unknit that threatening unkind brow . . .' (2.135–78) commands the Kate-impersonator. She argues from law of reason, civil law and the law of nature that women are biologically, culturally and necessarily inferior to men:

> I am ashamed that women are so simple
> To offer war where they should kneel for peace,
> Or seek for rule, supremacy, and say,
> When they are bound to serve, love, and obey.
> Why are our bodies soft, and weak, and smooth,
> Unapt to toil and trouble in the world,
> But that our soft conditions and our hearts
> Should well agree with our external parts?
>
> (V.2.160–67)

Petruchio has never heard himself speak so well.

Whereas before she became Petruchio's Tongue (whether in-cheek or not), Kate was sullen, dissatisfied, unamenable and unpopular, afterwards she is represented as radiant, powerful in utterance, a public success. Why then should we regret for Kate that she has lost the little matter of her own tongue – a mere three-inch flap of muscle in the chamber of a woman's mouth, inconvenient to society and of no practical use to herself?

Precisely for that reason: that it was *hers*. 'I could have lied,' reflects Amy Tan's narrator in *The Kitchen God's Wife*, 'and said, "Tonight the food is delicious." But if I didn't fight, wouldn't that be like admitting my life was finished?'

The history of criticism of *The Shrew* is dominated by feelings of unease and embarrassment, accompanied by the desire to prove that Shakespeare cannot have meant what he *seems* to be saying; and that therefore he cannot really be saying it. The play is ascribed with a crafty subtext to demonstrate that, for all its surface misogyny, the underlying message is subtly different, ambiguous or the direct antithesis of the obvious. Some say that this 'real' message is not just ambiguous but ironic; or that the play's romping farce and horseplay somehow reclaim its offensiveness by distancing it from the real and converting it into the carnivalesque or pantomimic. Others treat it as a fully developed romantic comedy comparable with *As You Like It* or *Twelfth Night* in which the major characters, including Petruchio, subtly grow, interact and achieve the equality of a true love-relationship. Another school reads Kate as a cloven, neglected woman in need of psychotherapy, which Petruchio, through game-play or role-play, provides. Some accept the notion of the subjugation of a woman by a man because it represents the prevailing ideology of a bygone historical period. Others highlight the Sly frame-plot to show that the viewer is placed at several removes, detached and distanced enough to see the Kate–Petruchio story as a play-within-a-play, an illusion or dream from which the Tinker emerges none the wiser. In this interpretation, the 'counterfeit supposes' of the Bianca plot, with its multiple disguises, become central in establishing the play as an arena of illusion. Two formidable apologies for the play come from the reading that sees Kate's acquiescence not as a lesson to the audience but as an exercise in Brechtian alienation, whereby debate is provoked in a sceptical audience; and from emphasis on a feminist subtext, which is held to work against the bias of the surface misogyny.

In all these programmes and projects, a common desire is discernible: to save Shakespeare's face. Performances of *The Shrew* tend to be exercises in rehabilitation, mediating the barbarous and primitive presentation of gender relations through adept manoeuvres intended to rescue the comedy from its own brutal ideology. Indeed, the persistence of directors and critics over, literally, centuries in reforming, rewriting, amplifying and defending *The Shrew* has an almost pathological quality.

43

In large part, this has been a reflex of bardolatry: the play must have value because Shakespeare wrote it. In part it represents a resistance to the fact of *The Shrew*'s anomalousness in the Shakespeare canon. For his plays show a steady, profound and moving allegiance to the image of women's integrity and intelligence, and an insistence on their oppression under patriarchy which runs counter to the conventions of the period. A modern critic has said that there was no such thing as feminism in Shakespeare's time and that she sees 'little evidence that he was ahead of his time in his attitudes toward women' (see Woodbridge, p. 222). I could not agree less. Most especially, women are seen as victims of the *tongue* of patriarchy: from Hero in *Much Ado* to Desdemona in *Othello*, Imogen in *Cymbeline* and Hermione in *The Winter's Tale*, women are presented as venomously slandered by the males who surround them and control their lives. At the same time, as I shall show later in this chapter, Shakespeare reclaims and rehabilitates the stereotype of the shrew or scold. Beatrice in *Much Ado* is 'my Lady Tongue', a fountain of wit and brilliance; the voice of the outspoken Paulina in *The Winter's Tale* is the tragicomic lash of penance and agency of deliverance. Read alongside these plays, *The Shrew* seems unShakespearian in its apparent acceptance of a misogynist ethic: a Punch-and-Judy show of great vivacity but questionable merit. Yet this is a curiously powerful Punch-and-Judy show, lit by flashes of wit and powered by the momentum of a sexual drive whose force makes for dynamic and exciting theatre.

In Daly's production of 1887, Ada Rehan played Katherina as, in the words of one critic, 'externally a virago, but the loveliest qualities of womanhood are latent in her . . . at war within herself; a termagent in temper; haughty; self-willed, resentful of control' but at heart coveting the submission which love will bring, and secretly in search of it. Her weakness, against which she rebels, is really her 'as yet unrecognized power' (see Winter, pp. 250–51). Here we glimpse a producer, an actress and a critic colluding to reinforce an oppressive social ideology which presents itself under cover of a standard psychological theory: the idea that women in conflict with their social roles are really in conflict with a sublimated 'natural' desire in themselves. Their autonomy is a denial of their need to surrender, for only in yielding do they paradoxically achieve power. George Bernard Shaw also viewed this production, a year later – with contempt. Picking up the reactionary project like one who has smelled a most unpleasant rat, he called it 'one vile insult to womanhood and manhood from the first word to the last' (see Haring-Smith, p. 69). Part of the malodorousness was explained by the fact that the production was heavily influenced by Garrick's revision:

Instead of Shakespeare's coarse, thick-skinned money-hunter who sets to work to tame his wife exactly as brutal people tame animals or children – that is, by breaking their spirit by domineering cruelty – we have Garrick's fop who tries to 'shut up' his wife by behaving worse than she ... In spite of [Petruchio's] winks and smirks when Katherine is not looking, he cannot make the spectacle of a man cracking a whip at a starving woman otherwise than disgusting and unmanly.

(G.B.S. in the *Pall Mall Gazette*, 8 June 1888, p. 11)

Whereas the original play exposed a mercenary woman-hunting and -hating society, Shaw felt that any attempt to soften it palliated those truths.

Ninety years later, in 1978, Michael Bogdanov's production carried this line to its most extreme conclusion. In a rivetingly violent, feminist production, Bogdanov's Padua was a meat-market where daughters were sold into potentially wife-beating marriages. Jonathan Pryce's Petruchio was at best a manic clown, at worst a psychopath; Katherina an assertive, intelligent woman resisting male domination up to the end, through a show of dumb insolence. Bogdanov's belief was that Shakespeare had built into *The Shrew* all the ideological resources by which a producer could make a feminist assault upon the viewers' assumptions. His version challenged and threatened audience complacency, seeking to make them shift uncomfortably in their seats, 'to the extent of asking the audience to sit up and be counted' (see Holderness, 1988, pp. 91–2). Kate invested the speech of capitulation with a superb literality which confounded its logic and ethics in the moment of speaking. When she reached its climax:

> And place your hands below your husband's foot.
> In token of which duty, if he please,
> My hand is ready, may it do him ease.

(V.2.176–8)

she actually placed her hand under his foot, whereupon he visibly recoiled from his own gratification. But such fierce expositions run directly counter to the reactionary surface project of *The Shrew*, with its deep roots in the patriarchal psyche. The jokes, whether lewd, sharp or barmy, endorse this spirit of reaction; and there is very little in the text itself to present an explicit criticism of the surface project or to provide the 'great speech' with a matrix of irony. Meryl Streep in the Delacorte production of 1978 was not at all embarrassed by the message she had to convey: 'What I am saying is, I'll do *anything* for this man ... Look, would there be any hang-up if this were a mother talking about her son? So why is selflessness here wrong? Service is the only thing that's important about love' (*The New York Times*, 6 August 1978, II, p. 5). This is acutely revealing, in excusing unilateral self-prostration by hooking it on to a relationship between unequals (mother and son), as well as unconsciously raising some rather interesting Oedipal questions about why males in our society feel the need to dominate over females.

The existence of a 'problem' such as that presented by *The Shrew* seems self-evidently to require a 'solution'. No one would dream of putting on a play which did not, either in intention or appearance, make sense or achieve a cogent kind of incoherence. This may of course be the involuntary impression left with us by a play, manifest in bad reviews, disgruntled audiences or even (as in a production I witnessed in the 1960s at the Manchester Contact Theatre) hisses or catcalls – not loud but deep – directed by the audience at Kate's oration. But no director stages a play which she/he considers to be radically unsatisfact-ory, with a view to displaying that unsatisfactoriness. For then she/he, as well as Shakespeare, has hazarded a hard-won reputation as well as soliciting the common-sense question 'But why put on the play in the first place if you consider it to be such a mess?' Hence, production is likely to attempt to resolve problems or offer solutions, to make the pointless and excrescent seem meaningful, and to amend undesirable elements by placing them in a frame or at an angle that distances or conceals flaws, whether moral or aesthetic. Production is *always* an art of *re*construction, and frequently of revision. Directors cut what is considered to be extraneous or liable to prove incomprehensible to the audience. One rarely sees a Shakespeare play in its complete form today: phrases chopped off here, whole speeches there, represent a form of unacknowledged censorship practised by all companies from the Royal Shakespeare Company to the local rep. Garrick's omission of the entire Induction to *The Shrew*, as well as the Bianca plot, plus his elaboration of Kate into a far stronger character who sets about reciprocally taming Petruchio, represents an obvious form of bowdleriza-tion. But, whatever you think of the resultant farce, at least it was honest bowdlerization, rather than silent suppression:

> Catherine shall tame this Haggard; – or if she fails
> Shall tye her Tongue up, and pare down her Nails ...

announces his heroine with a zest that symmetrically matches

Petruchio's, whom Garrick has tamed into a gentlemanly tease who finally marries Katherina for love rather than money. This symmetry exposes the asymmetry of the original, which makes Kate so much more susceptible to hurt and damage in her impotence against her manic tamer. When Planché and Webster restored the full play in 1844, it was in an attempt to recapture the authenticity of the Elizabethan staging, acting methods and conception.

There is an important modern school of thought which maintains that, because drama is a corporate activity, and good and bad quartos and Folio readings are so uncertain, no play-text is or should be sacrosanct. On the contrary, the words on the page (if and when the bibliographers have agreed them) are only the basis for a play, which is properly speaking an improvisation transacted between director, producer and actors. Texts are plural, open and indeterminate. But one does not have to be a die-hard follower of the old-school 'definitive' text, where the Folio is God, to insist that the script of a play advertised as 'by Shakespeare' can only be plural, open and indeterminate to a certain degree, this degree being a matter of common-sense judgement. A shrew or hawk cannot, for example, as I demonstrate on p. 88, be a duck or dove. To make common-sense judgements has become in some latter-day criticism an enterprise nearly as risky in opening one to ridicule as it was for Dr Johnson when he famously kicked the stone to test its reality.

However, although for the purposes of this study I am assuming that 'meaning' is not eternally 'elsewhere', in the case of *The Shrew* the full meaning is or was certainly somewhere else. For the text as transmitted in the Folio is not full and complete. Crucially the Chistopher Sly frame-plot, complete in the version *A Shrew* (hereafter referred to as the Slie frame-plot), whether an early or bastard version of Shakespeare's play, fades out after the two-scene Induction and the interpolation at the end of Act I, scene 1. Sly, having drowsed off to sleep in his drunken stupor, is awoken by his 'wife' and compliments the performance thus: ''Tis a very excellent piece of work, madam lady./Would 'twere done!' (I.1.250–51). These are his last words and he is thereafter forgotten. The frame becomes an inconsequential false start to a device as unsatisfactory as a parenthesis minus its concluding bracket. Most modern performances cobble (or 'restore') the remainder of the Slie frame in from the other play, a procedure which raises its own problems (see pp. 67–8 below) since, for all the claims which have been made for it by modern radical editors questioning the Shakespearian textual canon, *A Shrew* remains what Ben Jonson called *Pericles*, a 'mouldy play'

However, the fact that modern producers feel called upon to supply *The Shrew* with an appearance of the integrity it so signally lacks, demonstrates the degree to which *The Shrew* is a corrupt play in more than one sense. The Pirandellian use of the frame-plot used by John Barton in his famous *Shrew* of 1960, starring Peter O'Toole and Peggy Ashcroft, and followed up by Trevor Nunn in 1967, in which elaborate questions are asked about the relation between illusion and reality, seems to present a way out of the dilemma posed by *The Shrew*'s unsavoury ethos by suggesting that the core action is nothing but an illusion, as baseless as the 'supposes' of the Bianca plot, fabricated as a trick for the deceiving of a down-and-out by a troupe of poor actors. Nunn's programme notes commandingly put before his audience a 'Chinese-box' world in which vast questions were being implied:

When is anybody acting or posing, what do we accept and what reject, where is the basis of truth in this ever diminishing or ever expanding fantasy? It's a theme that Shakespeare never leaves ... It is only embryonic in *The Shrew* but it is excitingly and undeniably there.

Yet the Slie framework, which makes possible this bravura display of theatrical intelligence, is not even 'embryonic' in the play we have received under the title *The Shrew*: it is, rather, abortive. The frame in *A Shrew* has the virtue of being to all intents and purposes complete, ending with the awakening of Slie after 'The bravest dreame ... that ever thou/Hardest in all thy life,' to exit with the intention of applying its message by taming his own wife 'if she anger me' (p. 89). This device has to be patched into *The Shrew* in order to render it in the reflected light of the Shakespearian use of play-within-a-play techniques in *A Midsummer Night's Dream* and *The Tempest*. If any genius is 'excitingly and undeniably there', it is that of Nunn, not the Shakespeare of *The Shrew*. The issues raised are not dissimilar to those which arise in musical performance when, say, the earlier quartets of Beethoven are played *as if they were* late masterpieces: with hindsight, that is. No modern producer of *The Shrew* can take the play at its face value. It is presented to us retrospectively illuminated by borrowed glory and amended in the light of its source or acting version.

However inspired the creativity that informs these reconstructions, they are always responses to the feeling 'Shakespeare can't have meant it (can he?)'. I represent '(can he?)' in brackets in order to signal something of the half doubt that must ripple under the surface of the producer's confidence. He is in the business either of exposing or masking the reactionary power-relations of the corrupt sex that is the play's theme; pretending that the characters in the secondary plot are not as nondescript and verbose in their brainless disguises as they often seem (Tranio posing as Lucentio, Lucentio posing as Cambio, Hortensio posing as Litio, a pedant posing as Vincentio); mending the abortive framework and making the Lord's practical joke, which is the excuse for the whole action, more meaningful than an aristocratic oaf's boring prank. Often the dynamic casting of the lovers will carry the rest of the play along with it, dissolving the dubious morality in scintillating sexuality and hinting towards depths of characterization, which are stirred to mutual tenderness by the game of wit and will. Producer and actors have to milk every least hint of complexity for all it is worth. Thus in the Barton *Shrew* the superstar Peter O'Toole brought to the part of Petruchio a glamour of orgasmic virility which circulated into the role from his own legendary personality and life style; Peggy Ashcroft's sympathetic Katherina was a person aroused to love by the ferocious tempo of O'Toole's advances. The violence was legitimized by a triumph of acting that translated the power-relations into complex stratagems of sexual negotiation between male and female. In Zeffirelli's carnivalesque film (1967), explosive farce combined with the casting of Richard Burton and Elizabeth Taylor as the lovers to license the violent energies of a 'fantasy version of the Burtons' home-life' (see Holderness, 1989, p. 67).

In Jonathan Miller's television adaptation (1980), domestic sets based on Vermeer's Puritan interiors were the context for a naturalistic *Shrew*, which attempted to recapture a Tudor sense of the 'orderliness and grace and beauty of the family' (see Hallinan in Holderness, 1988, pp. 140–41). Petruchio's antics were viewed as a mode of psychotherapy for the tantrums of a neglected and hence disturbed elder daughter. Miller explained that modern medical practice prescribed ways in which 'a skilful therapist will gently mock a child out of a tantrum by giving an amusing imitation of the tantrum immediately after it's happened' (see Slater, p. 11). Petruchio apparently provides such a programme of rehabilitation, though how hysterical rampages can be viewed as the equivalent of gentle mockings passes my understanding. In this version, the idea of psychological healing covers up an unacknowledged political ideology. Conformity is viewed as a personal goal. Miller's interpretation brings into sharp relief the institutionalized bullying of the state in the form of its official or unofficial executive – be they husbands, psychotherapists, educationalists or the BBC – and the extent to which the normative, especially in a family context, is viewed as the measure of sanity, at the expense of the women and girls of the tribe. To the

49

question 'Shakespeare can't have meant it (can he?)', Miller replies to the effect, 'Well, yes, but only in the very nicest and most sensitive and benign sense.' And because the tone of Miller's voice and mind are invariably so thoughtful and intelligent, the play in his hands ends up perhaps more intrinsically sinister than as seen through the eyes of a less benevolent exponent.

Another escape route has been to stylize the acting methods so that mannered performance distances the events from reality and thus evacuates them from the realm of 'problem'. This liberates the audience from any ethical obligation, in the way that circus, pantomime, puppet shows and farce permit the wildest, but actually most ritualized, excesses in the name of pure exuberance and exhilaration. I mean 'pure' as opposed to 'applied'. For who would dream of springing up at a Punch-and-Judy show to denounce the politics of the conflict? Thus *The Shrew* may be played for entertainment value with minimal attention to the ethos. The *commedia dell'arte* style, with its masks, stock figures and precision choreography, has been a popular method of staging the comedy; a logical decision, since the technique returns the play to its roots in Italian comedy. In Act III Lucentio disguised as Cambio, commending his own suit to Bianca under cover of a Latin lesson, explains his extravagant proceedings as a means to 'beguile the old pantaloon' (1.36), Gremio, who is also described as '*a pantaloon*' in the stage directions following I.1.45. This designation attaches Shakespeare's play to the *commedia dell'arte* style, deriving from farce, in which the *pantalone* was a stock part, representing a foolish old man, wearing slippers, pantaloons and spectacles. Lucentio is identifiable as the *inamorato*, the young romantic lover who is destined to achieve the beautiful beloved. Harcourt Williams in 1931 played *The Shrew* as *commedia*, with brilliant Italianate costumes, masks, stylized gestures and poses, an interpretation which captivated critics, who found that the 'artificial atmosphere' transfigured 'the most churlish actions' (*The Times*, 14 October 1931, p. 10). The sharp and fast routines of farce also remove the action from the world of naturalism, as modish modern dress can also do: the 1920s modern-dress production by Barry Jackson in 1928, in which Tranio became the modern chauffeur of an on-stage automobile, is said to have had this effect. Farce was taken to its extreme in the 1930s, with the Lunts' circus stunt, the pretext for this extravaganza being that the taming play is no more than a diversion for a drunken tinker.

But if so, why put on the play at all? Does the audience wish to consider itself the intellectual equivalent of a drunken tinker? The

'Merrie-England' style of presentation, in which frisky lords might be conceived as springing harmless japes on stupefied peasants, is now as objectionable and old hat as the famous lecture celebrating 'Merrie England' in *Lucky Jim*. The introduction of the Sly plot as an intrinsic qualifier to the major action raises important issues, which I shall address separately (see pp. 77–84 below). The Sly material leads to twin and incompatible possibilities: either it reduces the taming action to an entertaining romp, denying the controversial pertinence of the themes, or it raises searching and uncomfortable questions about the relation between tinkers and lords, and males and females, within the social order – but connects the two in a way the poetry of this play is too thin to support. Bogdanov in a thrilling theatrical gesture augmented and extended the Sly contribution in his 1978 production by preluding the Induction with the outbreak of a loud quarrel in the auditorium between a drunken male and an apparent usherette, who turned out to be the actress playing Katherina. Part of the script for the drunk's harangue ran as follows:

You've done what? what have you done? You've sent for the police, have you? All right, you get the police, I'll wait here. Don't you bloody well talk to me like that, I've got every right to be in here. If there's anybody going to get sorted out around here, it's you, all right? You're not going to talk to me like that. All right, I'll wait right here, OK? You can't tell me what to do – no bloody woman's going to tell me what to do.

I'll wait here, OK? If there's anybody going to get sorted out it's you. OK, I'll wait here, go on, you go and get the police.

What's your game, chief? What's the matter with you? Look I've got no quarrel with you, it's just her. You talk to me like that, you bloody cow. Look, leave it out will you?

(RSC Prompt-book)

In this speech, Bogdanov has crystallized all the social discontent and violence that implicitly underlie the play's comic surface: the bellicose desperation of the underclass in the person of the drunk, who takes refuge in the bottle, defers out of fear to the male authority-figure ('chief') and takes out his deprivation on the woman. Clambering on to the stage, the drunk proceeded to demolish the whole set, an Elizabethan period illusion, to disclose a modern scaffold stage, where a new reality was constructed for a play the director had violently implanted at the heart of the reality inhabited by the audience itself. Bogdanov related the issues of class and gender oppression through the hunting motif used to exploit Sly and subject Kate, turning the play into a passionate condemnation of patriarchy and the class system. Asinine and arrogant lords hunt human foxes; the human prey passes on its injury to female victims. Merrie England becomes Murderous England, the Lunts' circus act a fierce indictment of capitalist blood sports. Yet, when we look from Bogdanov's vision back to the text of *The Shrew*, doubts arise. The director has felt compelled to make significant additions to the transmitted text, to bring home to his audience the implications of the action and the audience's implication in the system. Bogdanov has fly-posted the play, with augmentations, on a political notice-board, supplying his own induction to the Induction. It is only one further step to Marowitz's collage *Shrew*, which strips the narrative of decoration and fun down to its sordid basis in male sexual violence, crystallized in Kate's submission to anal rape by Petruchio:

If one peels away all those arbitrary layers of comedy and looks at the fable unadorned, one finds a play closer to *The Duchess of Malfi* than to *The Comedy of Errors* – a Gothic tragedy rather than an Elizabethan comedy . . .

the adaptor has written in a chapter of *Recycling Shakespeare* entitled 'How to Rape Shakespeare' (see Marowitz, p. 22).

When we turn from productions of *The Shrew* to the critical tradition, the adjustments made by the theatre to render the comedy palatable, coherent or challenging are given theoretical form. From their cultural elevation, academics have traditionally written in an andro-centric world in which even women have posed as honorary males. Apologists for *The Shrew* read the play standing on their hands with one eye closed; from this wobbly advantage they have felt in a position to tell us, *de haut en bas*, that black is really white. The student is required to accept on authority that misogyny is fair-mindedness, that the sun is the moon and that, when the Bard has fallen flat on his face, he is really up and dancing to a sublimely spirited tune. It can be said in favour of *The Shrew* that not only has it often brought out the worst in its critics but that it has done so in a peculiarly transparent way, evoking a discourse that moves inexorably towards self-parody. It bares the nerve of sexual controversy and exposes the depths of prejudice which most of our fellow-citizens keep hidden in the interest of common politeness.

The critics of whom I am thinking are the 'pantaloons' of the academic world, of antique vintage whatever their actual age. A perfect example will be on most students' and teachers' bookshelves in the form of the Arden edition of the play, edited by Brian Morris and published in 1981, reprinted throughout the 1980s and still selling as the best available text, incorporating, one is led to think, a respectable and reliable introduction. And, indeed, the editing, textual apparatus and textual introduction are exemplary. The literary critical section is, however, a farrago of misogynist assumption applied to *The Shrew* as if it and the play constituted exemplary good sense. Such 'pantaloonish' readings exercise a disproportionate effect on a readership coming to the play for the first time because not only are they fundamentally uncritical but they also constitute acts of verbal mastery that replicate in the critical field the dominance they celebrate in the literature. For they solicit the reader's deference, both to the voice of their own authority and to the message of the play, which they bless and authorize. They encourage the reader's mind to nod back into the elderly sleep of thousands of years of unchallenged ideology, in which it is comfortable for them to bask. Rather than awaken and alert the reader to ask disrespectful questions of the play, they mediate it as a learning exercise. Morris defends the Bard – and his stooge, Petruchio – as the fountain of wisdom. Katherina he dismisses as 'not particularly intelligent':

She simply reacts, violently, to stimuli. In this respect, too, she is like the animal: her reactions are 'shrewish' . . . Petruchio is the teacher, Katherina his pupil. His task is to inculcate such knowledge and instil such behaviour as will fit her to take a useful place in the existing society . . . it is significant that he never physically assaults or chastises her . . .

(Morris, Arden edn., pp. 124; 131; 132)

Morris here supplies Petruchio with a reference as teacher and husband. I for one am not impressed. Certainly the adept teacher does not whack his pupil, but neither is it generally considered matter for congratulation that the educationally minded husband refrains from corporal violence. And if Kate is trained to take a 'useful place' in society, one might want to ask to whom she is useful? The ideological programme Morris pursues is similar to that of Muriel Bradbrook when she defended the necessity of seeing people as 'merely a lawyer, a priest, a mother, a Jew . . . for practical purposes . . . Assigning and taking of roles is in fact the basis of social as distinct from inward life'. Petruchio's wholesome curriculum is reinforced by 'strong demonstrations of his natural authority' (see Bradbrook, pp. 132–50). That word 'Jew' echoes unpleasantly in relation to the idea of 'natural authority'. Women and slaves have always taken a 'useful place' in civilization: it is naturally troublesome to the civilized when the doormats rise up to demand rights, beginning usually with the right to be heard. Morris and Bradbrook's defence of the *status quo* has learned and applied nothing from centuries of class and gender conflict; and is determined to learn and apply nothing. Such criticism takes refuge behind the blinds of a Tillyardian historicism, in which 'what the Elizabethans would have thought' about social hierarchy usurps priority in judging the significance of a play.

Contrasting Petruchio with the deluded romanticism of Lucentio, Morris becomes rhapsodic at the thought that 'One thinks of Petruchio as somehow older than the other characters' (see p. 143). *One* thinks . . .? Who is 'one'? This formula exemplifies a familiar academic sleight that invites the reader into the club of intellectual privilege as a means of deflecting adverse criticism from the patent ludicrousness of the given statement. Petruchio is congratulated on his berserk performance as a form of wisdom and maturity qualifying him as a sort of pantaloon-to-be. Katherina's 'great speech' is defined as an unequivocal statement of the theory of 'degree' which Shakespeare 'meant to be a final statement on the subject of love and marriage . . . Shakespeare cannot possibly have intended it to be taken ironically' (pp. 145; 146). I notice that in the margin of my copy I have inscribed beside the latter statement the exclamation 'More fool him' (meaning, Shakespeare), and although I can imagine the point being made more felicitously this reaction seems to me to constitute a more seriously critical act than anything in the Arden introduction. Every reader and viewer should feel empowered to say of the Bard at some point, 'More fool him': otherwise the text becomes the funerary monument to an embalmed tyrant. No one would be more amazed than Shakespeare, I presume, at the questionable magnificence of this high and unsought office. The consummation of the pantaloonish reading comes in the critic's rapturous reception of Katherina's offer to place her hand below her husband's foot:

She is grateful for the delicate way in which he has handled the situation . . . She gives more than Petruchio asked. She gives full measure, pressed down, shaken together, and running over. And she ends by doing something that was never required of her . . . and quite gratuitously, she offers a public gesture of subservience freely and unasked . . . Petruchio responds to this unsolicited act of love and generosity with one of the most moving and perfect lines in the play, almost as if he is lost for words, taking refuge in action: 'Why, there's a wench! Come on, and kiss me, Kate.' I believe that any actor striving to represent Petruchio's feelings at this moment in the play should show him as perilously close to tears, tears of pride, and gratitude, and love.

(Morris, Arden edn., p. 149)

What a world of implication it is possible to read into a mediocre and indeed somewhat vulgar and boorish line, if that line happens to proceed from Shakespeare's pen. The same line in a play by Dekker or Beaumont would pass entirely unremarked. From Shakespeare's most tedious utterances clouds of glory are seen to trail. The 'tears' with which Petruchio is urged to welcome the subservience of his wife would represent the sentimentality of a ruffian, anathema to a self-respecting woman.

And, indeed, few modern critics have been able to stomach *The Shrew*'s last act with this straightforward relish. Shaw called it 'disgusting'; Quiller-Couch pointed out queasily that the plot was likely to be 'offensive' to modern women; Harold Goddard argued for an ironic reading of the 'great speech', in which Katherina, in allowing Petruchio to think he dominates her, will really be dominating him:

This interpretation has the advantage of bringing the play into line with all the other Comedies in which Shakespeare gives a distinct edge to his heroine. Otherwise it is an unaccountable exception and regresses to the wholly un-Shakespearian doctrine of male superiority, a view which there is not the slightest evidence elsewhere Shakespeare ever held.

(Goddard, p. 68)

The reason given for discrediting the surface meaning of this speech argues not from the work's internal logic but from the notion of what counts as truly Shakespearian, derived from the full range of Shakespeare's works, together with the dislike of anomaly, especially disreputable anomaly. But anomaly, which is a fact of life and art, cannot be dismissed simply by wishing. Besides, the solution seems to the present reader just as odious as the problem it displaces. The underhanded manoeuvre through which, by letting the husband think that he wears the trousers, the wife can rule him by petticoat-government, is demeaning to both parties. Any conspiratorial wink accompanying the speech endorses the *status quo* and turns speech, like kisses, into lip-service to a useful social lie.

The ironic reading of Katherina's final acquiescence can be just as clear a symptom of bardolatry as the straight reading. In astronomy an intellectual manipulation used to be current which was known as 'saving the phenomena': this meant that, if a scientific explanation obviously failed to fit the demonstrable facts, the astronomer might invent a variation on a discredited theory which closed the gap between hypothesis and data without renouncing the basic theory. Thus the Ptolemaic system in which the planets circled the earth was augmented by the invention of 'epicycles', whereby the heavenly bodies had to pedal furiously in minor circles *on* major circles in order to fit the observed facts. 'Saving the phenomena' in science was a face-saving resort tending inexorably to conservatism. Ironic readings of *The Shrew* have tended also towards a saving of the phenomena which is intrinsically reactionary, permitting the critic to evade the implications of the play's male-centred ideology. In this project, women readers have freely co-operated, partly out of devotion to Shakespeare for his powerfully sympathetic renderings of women characters in other plays. For Irene Dash, author of *Wooing, Wedding, and Power: Women in Shakespeare's Plays* (1981), Kate is 'an intelligent woman', 'a rational, observant woman' (see Dash, pp. 45; 49); Petruchio is admirable because he sensitively refrains from raping Katherina on their wedding night, but teaches her to join in 'high jinks', which initiate her into a 'gamesmanship' of great psychological value (see Dash, pp. 58–9).

Dash considers that Kate has come out of the shadows of familial neglect into a position of status and respect, has been wooed with sincerity and earned a champion and friend willing to pit her against all comers. In Act V, Kate takes the centre of the stage and wipes the floor with all her competitors through the ironic excess of her praise of male supremacy, in a witty language of reverse implication, learned from Petruchio. She has learned to *say*, that is, that black is white, moon is sun, while withholding her private opinion to the contrary. Towards the end of the chapter, Dash bursts out with a kind of throbbing, grateful emotion that we must judge Kate for ourselves:

Because he was a genius, because he could hear the words of women and transform them into language on the stage, because he did not filter these words through the screen of contemporary male prejudices, he was able to present vibrant, alive women. He recognised that women, like men, vary. He recognised women's humanity and immortalised it on the stage.

(Dash, p. 63)

The cart precedes the horse in the theatre of argument: 'Because he was a genius . . .' The three 'becauses' attempt to storm a citadel of disbelief that is particularly impregnable perhaps because it is built into the critic herself, in the form of private and unacknowledged doubt. Shakespeare is represented as a high-minded and sensitive proto-feminist, an escapee from the net of prejudice that is warp and weft of the human inheritance because it is woven into language itself. 'Because he was a genius . . .' But the author of *The Shrew* was not a genius. He was a somewhat more than averagely competent playwright with considerable stage skills, some finesse in the technicalities of complex plotting, a knack for bright verse-writing, and a terrific power to entertain. 'Because he was a genius': these five words wrong-headedly muzzle criticism and reinforce the right-mindedness of Ben Jonson's pointed exclamation: 'I loved the man, this side idolatry.'

Yet it would not be fair to ignore the fact that such critics are reacting to and attempting to integrate a genuine anomaly in Shakespeare's treatment of women's place and language, though Kate of *The Shrew* accords with the Kates of *Henry IV, Part One* and *Henry V* in being made mute, in having her tongue put down. But then Kate Percy, as a female in a martial history play, is always on the losing side; and Katherine of France speaks the French language, which has always been good for a laugh in our bigoted island. Elsewhere, however, Shakespeare takes apart the idea of female silence. Cordelia is a quiet girl. Yet her keeping of her own counsel rocks the system to its foundations and cracks her father's authority across at the centre of a state and a self he can no longer control. When asked for public expression of her filial love, she responds with a fierce parody of maidenly reticence:

CORDELIA Nothing, my lord.
LEAR   Nothing?
CORDELIA Nothing.

(King Lear, I.1.87–9)

Paradoxically, to insist on saying nothing in contravention of paternal authority becomes a form of shrewishness. Cordelia is a silent shrew. She has turned her social obligation to keep quiet into a *right* to silence, in allegiance to a higher duty. Her silence flouts her father's paternal authority and loses her a dowry. The image of integrity in this play attaches to the plain-spoken in the persons of the down-right Kent and Cordelia. At the apocalyptic moment after her death, as her father attempts to nurse her back to life, he persuades himself that he catches the wraith of her voice:

> What is't thou sayest? Her voice was ever soft,
> Gentle and low – an excellent thing in woman.
> (*King Lear*, V.3.270–71)

Again, and finally, Cordelia says nothing. And the death of her voice is attached by the wandering mind of her father, recalling her from a now everlasting exile, to the icon of 'soft,/Gentle and low' womanhood she once impersonated. Silence, then, has many meanings: it is a sign for compliance, resistance, evasion, surrender or dumb insolence.

In early and late comedies, Shakespeare's scolds say much and have much to be said for them. Adriana in *The Comedy of Errors* rants and rails because she is impotent to keep the love and attention of her husband. From the first, it is clear that Adriana, a jealous wife, is also envious. Just as every slave would like the prerogative of a master, so every wife covets the independence of a husband:

ADRIANA Why should their liberty than ours be more?
LUCIANA Because their business still lies out o'door.
ADRIANA Look when I serve him so, he takes it ill.
LUCIANA O, know he is the bridle of your will.
ADRIANA There's none but asses will be bridled so.
LUCIANA Why, headstrong liberty is lashed with woe.
　　　　　There's nothing situate under heaven's eye
　　　　　But hath his bound in earth, in sea, in sky.
　　　　　The beasts, the fishes, and the wingèd fowls
　　　　　Are their males' subjects, and at their controls.

(*The Comedy of Errors*, II.1.10–19)

Luciana spouts the received wisdom that relates the 'bridal' to a 'bridle' and woman's subjected situation within the social order to the God-ordained structure of a patriarchal Creation, which knew nothing of the eating habits of the female mantis, nor of the dispensability of the male in nature. Adriana, raging round the stage in pursuit of a counter-part who forever flees her, engages our amused sympathy. She knows, and says, that it's not fair, to which Luciana complacently replies that it's not meant to be fair. The system of natural law requires the existence of secondary citizens. But this play, which, like *The Shrew*, deals with the master–servant and husband–wife relationship, recognizes the adversarial conflicts within these pairings, which contradict their mutual interest and identity. *The Comedy of Errors* recognizes that some women wish they were men. The petticoated condition represents the confinement of a bridled ass.

'O that I were a man!' seethes Beatrice at the crescendo of *Much Ado About Nothing*, in defence of her slandered friend, the quiet Hero, put to shame and the social death of disgrace by poisoned male words. 'O God, that I were a man! I would eat his heart in the market-place' (IV.1.301–2). Benedick interposes, 'Hear me, Beatrice – . . . Nay, but Beatrice – . . . Beat –' (303; 306; 309), but Beatrice, 'My Lady Tongue', rants on. 'O that I were a man for his sake, or that I had any friend would be a man for my sake! . . . I cannot be a man with wishing, therefore I will die a woman with grieving' (312–13; 317–18). *Much Ado* displays the opposite side of the debate about the nature of woman to that espoused by *The Shrew*. The witty tongue of Beatrice is licensed by the play: she is Benedick's mate because she is his match, affinity and equal. The old argument that makes Eve the offspring of a crooked rib and the origin of human sin is reversed by Beatrice:

LEONATO Well, niece, I hope to see you one day fitted with a husband.
BEATRICE Not till God make men of some other metal than earth. Would it not
grieve a woman to be over-mastered with a piece of valiant dust?
To make an account of her life to a clod of wayward marl?
                                                  (*Much Ado About Nothing*, II.1.50–55)

Feminist pamphleteers had pointed out that whereas Adam was created out of dust, Eve had a higher origin, being the product of God's image, Adam. As the last of God's creations, she must also be the best, since he created in ascending order of excellence. *Much Ado* is absolutely permissive to the brilliance of Beatrice's tilting at the system; the play endorses her superiority. Don John, the source of the scandal, is a villain; Hero's father, Leonato, acts when under pressure as a credulous and violent patriarch; Claudio is a scoundrel at his wedding. These men are indeed clods of 'wayward marl'; they cannot even qualify as 'valiant dust' for, despite their military prowess, they are cowards, in flight from emotional reality. 'Men,' the song laments, 'were deceivers ever' (II.3.61). The recent Kenneth Branagh film, beautifully capturing the dappling of comedy and menace in the play, also celebrated the high spirit of the wit-contest between Beatrice and Benedick.

How then does one reconcile the licensing of the merry scold in *Much Ado* with the squashing of the sad scold in *The Shrew*? Partly, perhaps, it is a matter of development. *The Shrew* is an early play, certainly composed before 1594 and just possibly as early as 1589. We may also view the difference as one of class. Beatrice is a lady, with all the privileges belonging to the courtly class, including the intellectual privilege of education and the dignity of inheritance. She may be warned by Leonato that she will get no husband 'if thou be so shrewd of thy tongue' and Antonio may chorus 'In faith, she's too curst' (II.1.17–18) – but what's the odds? She doesn't want a husband. At least she alleges she doesn't, and appears to think she doesn't. The fact is, a husband is not an economic necessity:

BEATRICE Too curst is more than curst. I shall lessen God's sending that way;
for it is said, 'God sends a curst cow short horns', but to a cow too
curst he sends none.

LEONATO So, by being too curst, God will send you no horns.

BEATRICE Just, if he send me no husband; for the which blessing I am at him
          upon my knees every morning and evening.

                                (*Much Ado About Nothing*, II.1.19–26)

These words 'shrewd' and 'curst', which weigh so heavily upon Kate
that her whole identity is chained to them and she must clank them
wherever she goes, weigh as lightly to the high-ranking, liberal-hearted
Beatrice as balls to be juggled. By shrewdly playing upon her 'curst'
disposition, she retains the distance between herself and others as a
private space, which authenticates her identity as her own. That space
is the sanctuary of free speech. It is not economically imperative for
Beatrice to marry. *The Shrew*, however, is a bourgeois comedy in
which the woman's value resides in the price she will fetch: Kate is
her father's property who will be conveyanced to her husband as to
a new owner. Of the high-ranking Beatrice, it may be said that 'the
lady fathers herself' (I.1.102).

In the late play *The Winter's Tale*, Shakespeare develops the shrew
or scold character into an agent of destiny, with benign powers link-
ing her to art and white magic. In this revolutionary development of
the scold stereotype, the figure is moved to the threshold between
comedy and tragedy. As Paulina flays her king with her loud truth,
we hardly know whether to laugh or to cry. She comes to Leontes
bearing the baby Perdita in Act II, scene 3 'with words as med'cinal
as true' (37). Nothing will make her stop talking. Her truth is uncontrollable. Leontes mocks Antigonus for his inability to rule his preposterous wife. He who cannot rule his wife, Leontes sneers, is not a
man: 'thou art woman-tired, unroosted/By thy Dame Partlet here'
(74–5), 'He dreads his wife' (79). In other words, the henpecked Antigonus is a failed Petruchio 'That wilt not stay her tongue' (109), to
which Antigonus replies, in a quip that unerringly elicits a laugh
from the audience:

> Hang all the husbands
> That cannot do that feat, you'll leave yourself
> Hardly one subject.
>   (*The Winter's Tale*, II.3.109–11)

Yet even through our laughter, Paulina's dignity, loyalty and astringent
force of character impress us with a kind of greatness. As Hermione,
slandered, rises to her own resplendence at her trial in noble speeches
of self-defence which evoke our tears, so Paulina's impassioned

shrewishness in the same cause calls forth a tonic laughter, which goes to our hearts. Her tongue is an agent of Leontes' atonement and deliverance, as she awe-inspiringly brings the 'statue' to life in the final act: ''Tis time: descend; be stone no more . . .' (V.3.99). The shrew is no longer avoided as a public nuisance but courted as a source of truth guaranteed to be neither time-serving nor self-seeking. 'O grave and good Paulina, the great comfort/That I have had of thee!' (V.3.1–2): the voice of the honoured counsellor is that of the disobedient woman who will under no circumstances keep quiet.

When we move back from Shakespeare's development of the shrew or scold into a powerful voice of subversive wit in *Much Ado* and of subversive authority in *The Winter's Tale*, to reflect upon the taming of Katherina in *The Shrew*, the painfully reactionary character of the play's ideology moves into fuller focus. The girl's profound isolation and vulnerability come into relief, for she has no friend in the world, by contrast to the other heroines of Shakespeare's comic world. Shakespearian romantic comedy tends to provide a system of support and nurture for female individuals. Whereas Rosalind has Celia, Hero has Beatrice, Hermia and Helena did have and will have one another, Hermione has Paulina, and close female friendship is a norm, Kate has only Kate to stand up for Kate, against a world of money-grubbers, hand-in-glove relatives and 'subtle Dr Petruchio' practising the wild fandango of his so-called 'therapy' on her (see Nevo, pp. 48–9). That loneliness remains with me when the laughter of the audience has died away. It corresponds with an experience many dissident or anomalous women have endured and do endure daily in their lives; persons who are a joke to their neighbours and who are bullied by the community until they themselves see the joke. But what if the joke is your soul? Laughter is sometimes described as killing. Ann Thompson, the admirable editor of the New Cambridge edition of the text has written that 'In working on the play I have found that my own problem with its overt endorsement of patriarchy does not decrease,' though her respect for its craftsmanship and formal ingenuity increases (see Thompson, p. 41). Yet she too extenuates the play by comparing Petruchio (if played with the suggestion of sensitivity and intelligence beneath his brutality) favourably as a husband by 'most standards, even feminist ones' to the Orlandos and Orsinos of this world; and claims that the real problem lies 'outside the play in the fact of the subjection of women to men . . . It is the world which offends us, not Shakespeare'.

But this is manifest evasion. Take the bull by the horns. The bull *is* 'the world'. But the bull is also Petruchio, who reinforces through comic means a patriarchal programme we all recognize because we live in the world and see its manipulations and consequences. Society held the pen while Shakespeare wrote *The Taming of the Shrew*; he merely added various curlicues and embellishments; gave the bull an uproarious acting role and choreographed its rampaging hooves for a spectacular mating routine. If we are *not* offended by the tragedy of Shakespeare's comedy, there is something wrong: the offensive world has implicated us too.

4. The Strange Disappearance of Christopher Sly

The Shrew opens with a man threatening to beat a woman: 'I'll pheeze you in faith,' and the woman retaliating by threatening the man with the law: 'A pair of stocks, you rogue!' (Induction 1.1–2). On a first viewing or reading, it would be possible to mistake the woman for the 'shrew' advertised in the title, but, as it soon turns out, her indignation is the righteous outrage of a publican whose hospitality has been abused by a drunken down-and-out who refers to himself as a tinker but is denominated Beggar in the Folio. He now staggers around the stage in paralytic condition, refusing to pay for the glasses he has smashed in the hostelry, and shortly subsides into an alcoholic stupor. This is Christopher Sly, whose strange case is now to be investigated.

Sly is central to the Induction, a form Shakespeare never used in any other play. It lasts for two scenes and forms the pretext for the staging of the Paduan action as a play-within-a-play, put on by a troupe of strolling players at the behest of a whimsical lord, as an entertainment for Sly, to fool him into believing himself to be a lord rather than a vagrant peasant. Sly is the first example of comic transformation in a play of disguises and 'counterfeit supposes' (V.1.106), prefiguring the role-reversal between master and servant in the Bianca plot. The Induction is not perfunctory but extended and detailed, encouraging the viewer to feel that this is a major focus of dramatic interest. It introduces the themes of role-play, deception and illusion, not only in the transformation of Sly but also in the transvestism of the Lord's page, Bartholomew, who is instructed in how to play the part of Sly's supposed wife, and in the reception and briefing of the group of travelling players. The extension of the Induction into two scenes allows the playwright to develop the themes of rank and identity by having Sly awaken to his magically and mysteriously conjured status as a member of the aristocracy, a consumerist dream-world in which he is offered an honoured share in the surplus and excess of that lifestyle. From his base prose and pursuits he awakens to their Marlovian blank verse, studded with embellishment of classical mythology; from his habitual poverty and narrow aspirations, he succeeds to their menu of instant gratifications in a life that can offer rich array to one who has never owned more than one suit of clothes at a time – fine wine for beer, sensual delectation and artful luxury in place of an unaccommodated lifestyle.

But after the close of the Induction, when Sly and his boy-wife settle down to watch the play, he is heard from only once more, briefly, at the end of Act I, scene 1, when the Lord points out to him that he is not paying attention: 'My lord, you nod, you do not mind the play' (246), and his 'wife' remonstrates that it has only just begun. Sly props his eyes open with evident reluctance and manages a slurred compliment to the proceedings: ''Tis a very excellent piece of work, madam lady,' contradicted by his sincere grunt, 'Would 'twere done!' (250–51). The Folio stage direction, '*They sit and mark*', implies that Sly and his attendants remain on-stage as an internal audience. But they never speak again, nor does the play allude to them. Sly vanishes from the text of *The Shrew* without trace.

In a play of many embarrassments of a moral and political character, the erasure of Sly compounds the work's flawed nature by betraying a structural weakness which threatens subsidence to the whole creation. Did Shakespeare, having elaborated the beginnings of a frame-plot but growing bored with his drunken tinker, simply forget him? Was there some gross and unprecedented error of transcription, whereby the version Shakespeare wrote or the script used in the theatre only found its way into the Folio in aborted form? Or was it the dramatist's intention to present on-stage throughout the performance a sleeping audience, which would presumably be lugged off at the end still snoring? If so, why? And what is a modern producer to do about the unsatisfactory management of a stage device that was popular among playwrights at the turn of the 1580s and the early 1590s – the best-known and most effective being Thomas Kyd's *The Spanish Tragedy* (1592), in which the characters of the ghost of Andrea and the figure of Revenge (an audience observing from the 'other world' of the dead) witness the events throughout, and comment in the prologue, epilogue and between acts.

The conundrum is in some respects clarified and in others aggravated by the existence of a separate play printed in 1594 as *A Pleasant Conceited Historie, called The Taming of a Shrew*, in which a complete Christopher Slie frame-plot is sustained, with Slie presented not just as a prologue at a Warwickshire inn but placed in rhythmic relation with the taming action. Accompanied by the Lord, disguised as a servant, Sim, he comments and even intervenes, most notably when the Duke of Cestus, detecting the unauthorized marriage of his son, orders the lovers to be sent to prison:

SLIE   I say wele have no sending to prison.

LORD   My Lord this is but the play, theyre but in jest.

SLIE   I tell thee *Sim* wele have no sending,
To prison thats flat: why *Sim* am not I *Don Christo Vary*?
Therefore I say they shall not go to prison.

LORD   No more they shall not my Lord,
They be run away.

SLIE   Are they run away *Sim*? thats well.
Then gis some more drinke, and let them play againe.

LORD   Here my Lord.
    Slie drinkes and then falls a sleepe.

(*A Shrew*, pp. 80–81)

Here the framing device is fulfilling with considerable dexterity its ironical function of reflecting to the audience the self-consciousness of the play in reminding us that the people and events on the stage are only impersonations and illusions fabricated for the purposes of entertainment. Nobody in *A Shrew*'s Athens (rather than Padua, as in *The Shrew*) is going to be sent to prison, for, as Athens is a figment, so its prisons are painless and its people incapable of pain. Slie can be reassured on that count. However, he does not take the point: the idea of prison has hit a raw nerve and he repeats his objection, endorsing it by a reminder of his authority: 'why *Sim* am not I *Don Christo Vary*?' (a nearly phonetic seigneurial adaptation of his name Christopher). The answer to this would of course be, no, he's not Don Anything: his status and identity are just as illusory as the players' Athens, for he, who cannot tell a show from a reality, is in turn the victim of the Lord's deception. And the Lord, who is laughing up the sleeve of his disguise at having pulled a fast one on the 'slavish villaine' (p. 44), is also the actor of the part of Sim, who shushes Slie by reassuring him that the plot does not tend prisonwards and by pouring down his throat another draught of soporific ale. Conversely, however, in casting doubt on the Athenian action and Slie's perceptions, the frame-plot here reinforces the audience's impression of the reality of Slie as a poor fellow, duped. The actor playing Slie is not distinguished from his role. We feel that Slie – many Slies – do exist, outside on the street and at the receiving end of the boot of a publican, the truncheon of a policeman or the whim of the well placed. These people are not 'in jest'. We are also reminded by Slie's comically panicked intervention, 'I say wele have no sending to prison,' that Slie has probably in his time seen the inside of a jail, and no doubt will again.

The framing device is therefore used in *A Shrew* to considerable effect. Slie, catatonic, does not view the final scenes in which Ferando (the 'Petruchio' character) displays Kate's taming. The Lord has him dressed once more in his original rags and replaced in the lee of the alehouse where he was first picked up. Awakening after the players have left the stage, he glistens in the aura of 'The bravest dreame to night, that ever thou/Hardest in all thy life' (p. 89). He shambles off to put the taming lesson into practice on his own wife, thus ironizing the whole action by pushing it backwards into the frame of fantasy or dream, further away from the business of daily living. In its full-scale development of the Slie frame, *A Shrew* surpasses the premature dead-end of Sly in *The Shrew*, and because the poetic register of *A Shrew* is as a whole more primitive and heterogeneous than the glossy Shakespearian treatment, the bass notes of the Slie frame seem more in keeping with the mode of the whole. But here we strike against another problem, incapable of conclusive resolution. What is the provenance of *A Shrew* and how should it be read in relation to the Shakespeare comedy? There have been three major hypotheses. The first is that *A Shrew* was composed earlier than *The Shrew* by some other unknown playwright or collaboration of playwrights, and was used by Shakespeare as the source of his own play. The second is that both *A Shrew* and *The Shrew* derive from an original third play, an *Ur-Shrew*, which, like so many hundreds of plays written for the Tudor and Jacobean stage, has simply been lost. A third, and in our own century most popular, theory is that *A Shrew* is a memorial reconstruction of Shakespeare's play, a pirated text cobbled together by actors or spectators for printing and selling on the basis of the popularity of *The Taming of the Shrew*. It is thus what is called a bad quarto of the play, unauthorized by Shakespeare, which should be treated with scepticism. The latter view is taken by most modern editors.

Recently, however, a divergent way of viewing the relationship has been introduced (see Urkowitz in Charney, p. 204; Holderness and Loughrey, Introduction to *A Shrew*). Rather than disparaging the bad quarto as a corrupt pirated version of Shakespeare's authentic play as printed in the Folio, *A Shrew* is considered as an important document in its own right, with bearings on the Folio text. Holderness and Loughrey call *A Shrew* a 'Shakespearean Original . . . if not . . . a work by Shakespeare, certainly . . . a production of "Shakespeare" – the shorthand title designating a particular collaborative mechanism of cultural production' (Introduction, p. 17). In other words, the name Shakespeare, the signature of a unique historical individual, is expanded when cited in quotation marks to denote both the fluid conditions in which English Renaissance plays were created and to legitimate multiple texts. I might explain this by analogy: Shakespeare spelled his name when signing documents in a pleasant variety of ways. Spelling was not at that period fixed. It is now. Write 'Shakspeare' or 'Shakespear' in your essay and a censorious red mark appears in your margin. Neither was there a right or wrong text of *The Shrew*, *Hamlet* or *King Lear*, the argument goes: just different forms of 'cultural production'. Of course such a view is an irritant to readers, since our minds find difficulty in tolerating variance, and we shift from foot to foot in unease until disputes between right and wrong interpretations have been settled. Shakespeare, unlike Ben Jonson, did not prepare his own texts for the Folio edition, which was posthumous. What Shakespeare intended is necessarily hypothetical. And that intention becomes all the more conjectural when it is remembered that the texts, whose minutiae generations of scholars have scoured for exact meanings, were never composed as self-complete documents. They are closer to acting scripts, the basis for complex and dynamic theatrical events, decided together by playwright, director and actors. Late sixteenth-century plays were open rather than closed, relative rather than absolute: produced as scripts to be negotiated by a cast who had a say in how parts should develop and in the nuance and inflection of theatrical detail. Hence a bad quarto may be assessed on equal terms with a good quarto or the Folio.

So the argument runs. In the case of *A Shrew* there is especially compelling reason to take it seriously because this version encapsulates a complete Slie framework. If *A Shrew* is a memorial reconstruction, it may well be closer to the original written and staged version than *The Shrew*. If, however, the complete frame-plot has been introduced on no authority save that of personal inspiration into a bastardized text, then it has to be acknowledged that the author of *A Shrew* was in this instance a more competent dramatist than Shakespeare. So, at least, most twentieth-century producers seem to have felt, since they have tended to adapt the Slie frame from *A Shrew* into their productions of *The Taming of the Shrew*, filling in the gaping hole left in Shakespeare's text by his disappearing beggar and focusing the theme of theatrical illusion. This can do something to rescue the Kate–Petruchio plot from the charge of crude misogyny, and the Bianca–Lucentio–Hortensio plot from the charge of pointless disguises. However, the literary value claimed for the play by defenders of *A Shrew* is in my view unjustifiable. Though Holderness and Loughrey wittily take the Oxford Shakespeare editor H. J. Oliver to task for calling

Critical Studies: The Taming of the Shrew

A Shrew 'clearly inferior', its versification 'incompetent', its blank verse 'execrable', its diction 'slack', unfortunately these objections though rude are not at all ridiculous. Through the gloss with which he habitually polishes language, even in his less impressive works, Shakespeare unifies the discordant elements which in *A Shrew* present a medley of styles, varying from the coarse style exemplified in the exchange in the lute scene:

KATE   Then mend it thou, thou filthy asse.
VALERIA   What, doo you bid me kisse your arse?

(A Shrew, p. 58)

to the pseudo-Marlovian inflations of the wooers of Kate's sisters, Emelia and Phylema:

POLIDOR   Come faire *Emelia* my lovelie love,
          Brighter then the burnisht pallace of the sunne,
          The eie-sight of the glorious firmament,
          In whose bright lookes sparkle the radiant fire,
          Wilie *Prometheus* slilie stole from *Iove* . . .
AURELIUS Sweet *Phylema* bewties mynerall,
          From whence the sun exhales his glorious shine,
          And clad the heaven in thy reflected raies . . .

(A Shrew, pp. 59; 77)

Bad grammar (verbs which fail to agree with a noun) displays itself side by side with dim-witted cliché and tautology ('lovelie love'). The inflated rhetoric that is the play's major mode, characterized by grandiose hyperbole, extended decorative simile, embellishments of classical myth and exoticism, at once pillages and travesties Marlowe's *Tamburlaine*, *The Jew of Malta* and *Dr Faustus*. The effect of burlesque by the juxtaposition of the 'filthy asse'/'kisse your arse' style of colloquialism with Ferando's rough wooing of Kate, has a comic though limited parodic effect. An impression of woodenness in speeches and repartee contrasts with the greater fluidity and surface sophistication of Shakespeare's play, which smooths the decorative embellishments towards the naturalistic, and creates the semblance of unity of tone throughout the work.

However, without grafting the Slie frame on to *The Taming of the Shrew*, Shakespeare's play, for all its greater polish, makes incomplete theatrical sense. John Barton in 1960 and Trevor Nunn in 1967 showed what could be done when the frame and its implications are imaginatively exploited to focus the illusion and deceit which are the basis of the art of acting. Acting becomes not the means of production but the subject of exploration. Nunn's interpretation presented a drama about drama, in which the audience was rarely allowed to forget that the taming plot was a play-within-a-play, performed by a troupe of free-lance actors who had assumed their roles for the duration and were to shed them when the play was over. In Barton's production, a revolving stage slid round to reveal the inside and outside of a dilapidated Tudor inn, incorporating also a makeshift green-room in which actors could be seen changing costumes. In the midst of playing, they would fumble for their lines and require the services of the prompter. From balconies and windows, people watched the show, coming and going. Sly was a constant presence, clambering between a number of vantage points to command a better view, intervening and commenting upon the play as if it were (as to him it became) real. The effect on the Kate–Petruchio plot was, a reviewer reported, such as to transform 'a cruel and loutish farce into a light-hearted, charming comedy' (see Marshall, 1962, p. 312). The entire balance had shifted, the illusion of reality being focused on Sly as an inner audience. At the end, the cast all abdicated their roles and displayed themselves as the persons they had always been under their disguise of impersonation. But this exposure wittily generates another level of illusion, of course, in that these same 'real people' can only be (to us, the audience) always and only representa-tions, simulations. A theatre company has been playing the actors who play the roles. We the audience observe an internal audience (Sly) watch a play while also acting an unconscious part in a play he does not suspect or comprehend (his role as a lord).

The completion of the frame integrates the Induction with the central play by setting and maintaining in relief the theme of rank and class inversions, their instability and the covert mutual aggression and overt exploitation implicit in the dynamic of the master–servant relationship, which parallels the violent heart of the sex war. If *The Shrew* articulates and legitimates prejudice, its comedy also permits the voice of the underclass to become audible, as the 'inferiors' assume the trappings, speech habits and luxuries of their aristocratic or mercantile 'betters'. Role-reversal between classes is a norm of the play. Lucentio's 'man', Tranio, emulates and speaks for his master, outbidding his rival for Bianca with argosies of wealth (II.1), generating worlds of fictional ancestry out of his own conjuring brain-box:

> I see no reason but supposed Lucentio
> Must get a father, called supposed Vincentio.

69

> And that's a wonder. Fathers commonly
> Do get their children; but in this case of wooing
> A child shall get a sire, if I fail not of my cunning.
>
> (II.1.400–4)

When the real Vincentio arrives at Padua, he is scandalized to view his son's servant's spawn of a 'supposed Vincentio' (Biondello) but all the more so to survey the ostentatious get-up of this 'supposed Lucentio':

O fine villain! A silken doublet, a velvet hose, a scarlet cloak, and a copatain hat! O, I am undone, I am undone!

> (V.1.58–9)

Thy father? O villain, he is a sail-maker in Bergamo.

> (68–9)

The language of clothes depends on a dress code that was still in Shakespeare's day hierarchically and systematically precise, enshrined in law as the medieval Sumptuary Laws, enacted to restrain excess expenditure on clothing, food and equipage. Different garbs were prescribed for each rank in society, from headgear to stockings. But in an age of social mobility, where the lower classes attempted to lift themselves by all shifts into the rank above them, the dress code was confounded by widespread impersonation and 'disguise'. The vulgar could act the parts of their betters by assuming their costume. The Tranio–Lucentio reversal presents a visual metaphor for such threatening play-acting. Hence Vincentio's hysteria on viewing the villain-villein manservant done up in a sumptuous doublet of silk, his legs made of velvet, cloaked in scarlet, his head transfigured by the conspicuous splendour of a hat shaped like a sugar-loaf. A 'fine villain' is a walking oxymoron, a contradiction in terms, and yet the upstart villain does walk, most substantially, on his oxymoronic velvet legs. This vision undoes Lucentio's father because the pretender's father was no more than 'a sail-maker in Bergamo'. The fiction that wealthy dynasties transmit persons of blue blood is endorsed by the legalized fiction that their babies arrive pre-packaged in silk and velvet, while the lower orders come into the world in worsted. Petruchio's chaotic outfit in the wedding scene violates the dress code in the opposite direction, drawing attention to the arbitrariness of the sign-system in his 'To me she's married, not unto my clothes' (III.2.116).

The Shrew dallies with the notion that the dress code and name code are meaningless: that we are all (excepting women) when stripped naked made of the same material. Master and man are interchangeable.

But these suggestions are always essentially unthreatening to the established order because they remain on the level of comic 'supposes', 'flattering dream or worthless fancy' (Induction 1.42), which is staged for a laugh and to beguile the time of those who have nothing better to do (the Lord; the audience). Power-relations are exposed but not essentially challenged. Sly staggers on to the stage to transmit an inflated claim to noble dynasty as he hollers to the hostess, 'Y'are a baggage, the Slys are no rogues. Look in the Chronicles, we came in with Richard Conqueror' (Induction 1.3–4). If all humans are of ancient ancestry, whether beggar or tycoon, that levelling thought is further enriched by the cloudy character of history to an illiterate beggar. The difference between William the Conqueror and Richard Coeur de Lyon can be of merely academic interest to most of us, and particularly to a beggar whose own name is forever taken in vain. No more Gallic than a Smith or a Bloggs, a Sly's pretensions to high lineage stir a faint fantasy able to bring some warmth to the cold extremities of a vagrant, whose lack of possessions may be privately interpreted as a dispossession, and whose namelessness evokes the dream of a high name now perished, at some remote date. Sly, who is a nobody, never expects to become a somebody, but gratifies himself with fantasies of lofty lineage lost in antiquity. The beggar's illiteracy – mouthfuls of mangled Spanish ('*paucas pallabris*' (5)), muddled oaths ('by Saint Jeronimy' (7)) – expresses his excommunicated state in relation to society, chewed up and spat out. Sly challenges the powers that be from a position of gormless impotence, fighting with no other weapon than drunken bravado as many constables as may be sent out to control him: 'Third, or fourth, or fifth borough, I'll answer him by law' (11–12). He falls dead asleep and wakes to find his wildest imaginings ironically gratified.

With the Lord enters what we might call the Elizabethan Dream, equivalent to the modern American Dream but less materially accessible. One might ascend the ladder of privilege to become a gentleman, as Shakespeare was to do on the proceeds of these plays, accumulating wealth sufficient to purchase a coat of arms and the right to call oneself a gentleman; one might become a lord only by dreaming. The Lord has no personal name allocated to him by the economy of the play. He is nobody *in particular*, but a representative person of quality, a 'have' over against that insignificant but not anonymous 'have-not' flat out before him. Where Sly was hard up for meaningful expressions, the Lord is a big-talker and, when he talks, everyone else has to listen. The Lord enters fresh from the hunt, scattering commands in the blank verse suited to his rank, discussing the relative merits of his hunting hounds, of which a meritorious handful are named – Merriman, Clowder, Silver, Belman and Echo. The dogs are spoken of with respect and distinguished against one another as articles of value. Predatory noise is the specialism of the pack: like master, like dog. In full cry, they give tongue in the chase, and the 'deep-mouthed' (16) are the most in demand. Belman, says one of the huntsmen, is as good a hound as the Lord's favourite, for 'He cried upon it at the merest loss' (21), that is, he was still baying for blood (or 'belling', the technical term from which his name derives) when the scent had been lost. Now the Lord and his human dogs spy new prey. Affronted by the repellent sight of the gross Sly, the Lord exclaims:

> O monstrous beast, how like a swine he lies!
> Grim death, how foul and loathsome is thine image!
> Sirs, I will practise on this drunken man.
>
> (32–4)

If the abject animal has reminded the Lord of a hog, the hog has recalled him to his favourite pastime – hunting. The Lord now works himself up into a lather of excitement by priming his minions in how they are to act out their hoax. He directs the set (his best chamber, adorned with 'all my wanton pictures' (45)), background music, gesture and mien of the cast; he improvises an acting script ('Say "What is it your honour will command?" . . . And say "Will't please your lordship cool your hands?"' (52; 56)).

When the troupe of players arrives, their reality is authenticated by their reception as actors the Elizabethan audience might have seen in a well-known recent play (81–7). But the actors too are hoodwinked by the hunter-director into believing that their audience will include a real lord, whose fantastic behaviour will be explained by the fact that he is insanely innocent of plays (91–7). Finally, the Lord arranges a sex change. His page, Bartholomew, is to get himself up as a woman, Sly's supposed wife, the kind of wife Katherina will never be: 'With soft low tongue and lowly courtesy' (112). The application of an onion is prescribed if the boy finds his tear-ducts incapable of secreting feminine tears to welcome 'her' 'husband' back to the mainland of sanity from his years of derangement. The effect of this impersonation would have been to draw attention to the fact that the women in an Elizabethan play were impersonated by boys like Bartholomew, of tender years and treble voice: there was a budding phallus under the skirt, incipient bristle beneath the maidenly cheek and a moustache biding its time above the mouth that is directed to bestow 'tempting kisses' (116) upon that boor and boar, the Bartholomew-wife's cozened Sly-husband. Mature Shakespearian comedy would go on to reflect upon the mercurial homoerotic potential of its transvestite medium in a sequence of boy–girl heroines (Rosalind, Viola, Julia, Portia, Imogen), and even tragedy alludes to the sexuality of its illusions (Cleopatra's contempt for the stage versions of her grand action: 'Some squeaking Cleopatra boy my greatness' (*Antony and Cleopatra*, V.2.220)). But *The Shrew* leaves the motif in suspension, having provoked a snigger from the audience in the second scene of the Induction, where Sly wastes no time or ceremony in instructing his 'wife' to undress for bed, but is left 'standing' by Bartholomew's prevarications (Induction 2.117–26). This sexual ambiguity exerts no obvious tension on the misogynistic treatment of Kate in the inner play, though it is possible that the prevailing slapstick and farce would be reinforced by the burlesquing effect that a boy actor might give to Katherina's loud refusal of femininity.

The Induction presents the hostile extremes of Tudor society in a situation of folkloric exchange, closely related to the folk-tales still surviving of the prince-and-beggar reversals. But whereas in such tales the prince gets a taste of how the rough life of a down-and-out child might feel, taste and smell, traffic in *The Shrew* is one-way, with the Lord secure in his mastery and privilege. The focus of interest centres as much on the means of enacting illusion as on the conflict of classes, and thus not only evades painful issues of justice but urges its audience to share in unjust attitudes. The play does not ask us to evaluate the Lord's behaviour, though directors have chosen to do so: witness Bogdanov's brilliant costuming of the Lord and huntsman in the bloody arrogance of hunting-pink, dropping a gory fox pelt over Sly's prostration and thereby emphasizing his status as a victim, paralleling the goading and trapping of Kate. The wager scene in which Petruchio and the fraternity fly their 'birds' was also characterized in Bogdanov's production by the sound of hunting horn and hound. Petruchio plays the lord to his chattel as the Lord pursues his human game. Yet the text itself scarcely furnishes more than odd hints towards this integrating critical strategy. *We* may know that the Lord is a fatuous ass but that is not because the play tells us so. His homoerotic interest in the ambivalent boy-wife and 'her' swine-husband may seem to us like the perverted manipulations of a degenerate, but nothing in *The Shrew* explicitly endorses our disgust. On the contrary, we are supposed to be entertained by a collusive lord's-eye view:

> I know the boy will well usurp the grace,
> Voice, gait, and action of a gentlewoman.
> I long to hear him call the drunkard husband,
> And how my men will stay themselves from laughter
> When they do homage to this simple peasant.
>
> (Induction 1.129–33)

For this after all is what we came to the theatre to enjoy: pipsqueak boys miming grown women and underpaid actors playing to the galleries. Doing *homage* to a *peasant* is taken to be as self-evidently hilarious a reversal as lads in drag lisping wifely obedience to the jumped-up dregs of society.

In the second Induction scene, Sly awakens and immediately calls for a hair of the dog that bit him – 'small ale'. A barrage of offers presses upon him, of canary wine ('sack'), candied fruits, choice of apparel (Induction 2.1–4). Sly's prose honourably disclaims the right to be called 'honour' or 'lordship' (5–6), his palate being innocent of sack or sweets, his wardrobe being on his back, far gone in tattiness and subject to holes. The Lord's poetry tempts Sly to delusions of grandeur. Sly's homespun prose again authenticates his ragged state; gives his rough credentials:

Am not I Christopher Sly, old Sly's son of Burton-heath, by birth a pedlar, by education a cardmaker, by transmutation a bear-herd, and now by present profession a tinker? Ask Marian Hacket, the fat ale-wife of Wincot, if she know me not. If she say I am not fourteen pence on the score for sheer ale, score me up for the lyingst knave in Christendom.

(Induction 2.16–23)

Barton-on-the-Heath, a village near Stratford where an aunt of Shakespeare's lived, makes a Warwickshire man of Sly; his curriculum vitae denominates him a jack of all trades (though the Folio names him Beggar, there is no obvious reason to discredit his life-account). Marian Hacket, learned annotators tell us, was 'probably a real person' (see Arden edn., p. 163, n.) living in the hamlet of Wincot, four miles south of Stratford. Such local colour, setting Sly near his own regional roots, was perhaps Shakespeare's private joke. The point is that Marian Hacket sounds real; she sounds solid and substantial, fully fleshed. We feel that we could visit her, just round the corner from the theatre, where the path of the play becomes the road in the real world, and take up Sly's references. She would volubly vouch for him as a genuine knave and swindler, 'fourteen pence on the score for sheer ale' (or possibly more). The sheer prose of Sly works to endorse him as a real and really poor person. Then art can undermine his sense of reality and his comprehension of his identity, which is entirely dependent on class. In this sense, the bamboozling of Sly seems to intend a partial parallel with Petruchio's assault on Kate's grip on reality ('be it moon, or sun, or what you please' (IV.5.13)) – though she of course is not deceived.

'O noble lord,' solicits the ignoble Lord, 'bethink thee of thy birth' (Induction 2.29). He offers sensual delectations of an extravagance unimaginable by a card-carrying tinker: a consort of nightingales; a plump couch more voluptuous than that upon which the sexually voracious Queen Semiramis acquitted herself; the full red-carpet treatment, together with a go at those sporting recreations that dominate the play, of hawking and hunting (35–45). Who is this Semiramis, the Beggar might well wonder, this Adonis, Cytherea, Io, Daphne and Apollo whose names come up when the Lord's art-works are proffered? They live in another world than that of Christopher Sly and Marian Hacket. These pictures are evidently the Lord's erotic aids, with which he indulges himself in private, Ovidian portrayals of metamorphoses, featuring the rapes by Jupiter and Apollo of mortal maidens and prefiguring in rarefied form the sexual violence that characterizes the inner play (see Garner in Charney, p. 108). The art-works aestheticize rape in a manner familiar to Elizabethan visual and literary art, but the emphasis falls on the beguiling lifelikeness of the representations of Io before her rape, Daphne evading hers, 'Scratching her legs that one shall swear she bleeds,/And at that sight shall sad Apollo weep' (57–8). Artistic displacement of hymeneal blood and seminal fluids into a decorative blood drop pricked from a leg by a thorn and a golden god's shed tear leads from life into art, only to circle back from art to the semblance of life by insistence that this counterfeiting is so perfectly realistic as wellnigh to step from the frame of art and into the room. These old stories relate hunting to the sexual chase; they are the bait to catch the Beggar. We recall how deeply hunting penetrates into Western culture from its origins: the blood-lust is at the heart of 'civilization' and looks down at us still from a thousand Elizabethan paintings and murals as the essence of the 'cultured'. The Great Hall at Hardwick is dominated by a running frieze on three walls of an account of Actaeon, the hunter transformed into a deer by the punitive Huntress, Diana, and dismembered by his own hounds. The Beggar of Shakespeare's comedy is 'had' by a caste that puts a high premium on the art of hunting and hunting as art.

The Lord's art-works as described by his entourage are testimony that leads into the introduction of Sly's 'lady', that lustrous beauty

Bartholomew. Now the Beggar is precipitated into one of the few genuinely moving moments of the play. Bottom is translated. Sly awakens to the knowledge of his own magnificent estate, at first tentatively, pondering the evidences, then with certitude, which ripens without ado into the determination to enjoy himself:

> Am I a lord and have I such a lady?
> Or do I dream? Or have I dreamed till now?
> I do not sleep. I see, I hear, I speak.
> I smell sweet savours and I feel soft things.
> Upon my life, I am a lord indeed,
> And not a tinker nor Christophero Sly.
> Well, bring our lady hither to our sight,
> And once again a pot o'th'smallest ale.
> (Induction 2.67–74)

The poignant tickling sensations of humour in the reader or hearer of these lines are evoked by the change of register. The Beggar's vulgar prose is shed with his rags: having assumed the high-class mantle of blank verse, he reasons his case in simple terms; then, when he has concluded, he swells into the royal plural, tumbling into amiable bathos by demanding another pot of cheap ale in his last line. Sly has been asleep, so they tell him, for fifteen years, 'a goodly nap' as he observes (80), during which time he would refer to persons such as Cicely Hacket, Stephen Sly, old John Naps, Peter Turph, Henry Pimpernell. These vernacular English names, with their evidencing of reality, have now been called into comic question. As Adonis and Cytherea step out of the picture frame, winking, Cicely Hacket and Stephen Sly bundle out of the window. Fiction and reality change places. Sly is made ready for the play, equipped with a 'wife in all obedience' (106). But what is her name?

SLY   What must I call her?
LORD   Madam.
SLY   Al'ce madam, or Joan madam?
LORD   Madam and nothing else, so lords call ladies.
SLY   Madam wife . . .

(107–11)

Like the Lord, the Lady has no individual name, only her title. In the absence of such names, Sly suggests a couple, using her honorific as a kind of surname, 'Al'ce madam . . . Joan madam?' The Lord explains that the upper crust don't crudely buttonhole one another; their address is ceremonious. Sly can't get the hang of this at all. 'Madam' swims out of his reach in the Great Beyond of élite manners and mores. Finally he catches it on a hook which all classes of men understand, coupling 'madam' to 'wife'. For 'wife' is at the command even of impotence.

Or so he thinks. The text sniggers and signs to us behind his back.

If the Slie frame is cobbled into *The Shrew* from *A Shrew* and retained on-stage throughout, the director has a better chance not only of distancing and ironizing the taming action by enclosing it in the world of the fictive and questionable, but of highlighting the master–servant relationships of the play-within-a-play and raising them as questions of power and authority that parallel the gender problem. The role-reversals (*suppositi*) of the Bianca action may also be brought under the umbrella of the thematic deception being practised upon Sly. Lucentio and his man, Tranio, enjoy an affable relationship as a hand-in-glove pair, in which 'My trusty servant well approved in all' (I.1.7) can profess a budding acquaintance with the ancient philosophers and poets and feels able to advise a course of erotic and agreeable studies: Ovid, whose *Metamorphoses*, pictured in the Induction, will be echoed in the wooing changes of the Bianca plot, and whose well-thumbed salacious *Amores* were the Renaissance lover's textbook, in preference to the stuffy rigour of Aristotle. This epicurean advice is naturally congenial to the young master. Sly (if he has not already nodded off as in the Folio version) will now be viewed by us watching Lucentio and Tranio stand aside to watch the uproar as the Minola family and the suitors are introduced; he will see the hatching of the disguise plot as, having fallen in love with Bianca, Lucentio abdicates his class and identity (and class *is* identity in this play):

> Then it follows thus –
> Thou shalt be master, Tranio, in my stead,
> Keep house, and port, and servants, as I should.
> (I.1.198–200)

> Tranio, at once
> Uncase thee, take my coloured hat and cloak.
> (203–4)

The coding of social identity is undone and, just as Sly, stripped of rags, has been promoted to silks, Tranio's extempore quick-change usurps an attire and lifestyle to which he has no born right, only the comic obligation asserted by his master's command: 'I am tied to be obedient' (209). Playing on the idea of 'service' to one's mistress, Lucentio figures his precipitous downward mobility as a testament to his prostration in the cause of love:

TRANIO I am content to be Lucentio,
        Because so well I love Lucentio.
LUCENTIO Tranio, be so, because Lucentio loves.
        And let me be a slave t'achieve that maid
        Whose sudden sight hath thralled my wounded eye.

(213–17)

The Marlovian play on Lucentio's name focuses the eternal absence of reciprocity built into the master–servant relationship. Tranio croons his 'love', meaning the allegiance of a good servant; Lucentio replies with his own statement of love – for a woman, to whom he is a 'slave', 'thralled', in the conventional Petrarchan love jargon, Cupid's dart having pierced his eye and brought him low.

Biondello enters and gapes. Clothes are the man, so where is Lucentio? Regaled with his own absence, he points out the impropriety of such a question from someone who is not there: 'Where have I been? Nay, how now, where are you?' (219–20). Foul Sly had become silken Sly under the Lord's machinations: 'Wrapped in sweet clothes, rings put upon his fingers,' taught to 'forget himself' (Induction 1.36; 39). Lose your costume, lose your self. And yet the parallelism lacks bite in Shakespeare's play; it fails to persuade us that a unifying idea weaves these layers of meaning into a single and meaningfully comic pattern. Convention remains at the level of convention. Verbal parallels are not intense or striking enough to convince, as they do in *The Comedy of Errors* or *A Midsummer Night's Dream*: a kind of heterogeneous miasma prevails, intimating patterns that thin away on scrutiny to nothing, or not much. The Lucentio action seems to generate fabrications for their own sake, as Lucentio goes on to improvise a pack of lies for Biondello's benefit, to the effect that Tranio has adopted his costume to save his life from retribution for a murder he invents. Biondello comprehends the hoax as little as we applaud it. 'You understand me?' asks Lucentio dressed as Tranio:

BIONDELLO   I, sir? Ne'er a whit.
LUCENTIO And not a jot of Tranio in your mouth.
        Tranio is changed into Lucentio.
BIONDELLO The better for him, would I were so too!

(I.1.232–5)

This tart reminder that all servants desire to change places with their masters and mount in the social scale makes explicit what is implied but muffled in the Lucentio plot: the antagonism between classes, in a

78

hierarchy which is based on force, the rule of the strongest. Petruchio, like a rip-roaring big-talker from Aristophanes' Old Comedy, will come on demonstrating this universal truth in a display of arbitrary violence as he roughs up his servant, Grumio.

Both plots endorse the *status quo*, though they also act out the conflict within the class system at a time when unemployed servants formed a large vagrant class; materialism and individualism were eroding social certainties, and the servant's status as employee was at variance with his role as family retainer. Nostalgia informed the Tudor view of the love-relationship between master and man which 'was in maner equall with the Husbandes to the Wyfe, and the Childes to the Parent' (see 'J. M.', *A Health to the Gentlemanly profession of Servingmen*, in Moisan, p. 280). *The Shrew* reflects the blurring of class distinctions in the exchangeability of Tranio and his man, as well as the comic disobedience of Grumio to Petruchio's order to 'rap' him here (I.2.12), on the grounds of higher duty (servants must under no circumstances 'rap' masters). The love-languishing Lucentio rests on Tranio as on a cushion; the fiery and physical Petruchio pummels Grumio like a punch-bag. Both plots raise the ghost of possible revolt on the part of the servant class but in both it is laid as soon as raised. The well-oiled Tranio sleekly pursues his master's interest as his own, in mock-heroic rhetoric that apes the upper-class tapestry of rich words and classical allusions, displaying the gift of the gab that is a mark of class and sexual potency in the play: 'What, this gentleman will out-talk us all!' moans Gremio as Tranio presents his credentials as an extra wooer by pointing out the precedent of Helen of Troy who had a thousand (I.2.245; 240–44). Tranio is an actor and impersonator, who maintains his role right through to the climax, demanding that the true Vincentio be removed to prison as an impostor. He sits at table on fraternally equal terms with Petruchio in the final act, bantering about Lucentio's having slipped his huntsman's leash to wife-hunt on his own account (V.2.52–3).

Petruchio's servants, on the other hand, are scuttling targets for his fist and boot, and, though Grumio stands in for his master to torment Kate by tempting and disappointing her appetite (IV.3), he is among the crew of unfortunates who are madly whacked and insulted by their employer as he settles his bride in her new abode:

PETRUCHIO   Where are my slippers? Shall I have some water?
             Come, Kate, and wash, and welcome heartily.
             He knocks the basin out of the Servant's hands

> You whoreson villain, will you let it fall?
> *He strikes the Servant*
> KATHERINA   Patience, I pray you, 'twas a fault unwilling.
> PETRUCHIO   A whoreson, beetle-headed, flap-eared knave!
>
> (IV.1.139–43)

Petruchio's abuse of his knaves is an object-lesson to Kate in her husband's mastery of 'what is mine own' (III.2.228). His expression of tender and polite concern for her welfare is in a rapid rhythm of violent contrast with his assault on the servants. He professes objection not only to their clumsiness but to the sexual manners of their mothers ('whoreson' means 'son of a whore'), the unjustifiable shape of their skulls and the aggravating character of their ears. They hurtle and duck their way around the stage, pursued ultimately by the entire contents of the table, which Petruchio flings at them, on the pretext that the mutton is burned. Petruchio's ironic 'hearty welcome' is predicated upon the contradiction between his words to Kate and his deeds to them, which prevent them from serving her with the means of hospitality. Peter's 'He kills her in her own humour' (166) is not exactly to the point. For Petruchio's role-play enacts his own legitimate mastery. Kate could never reply in kind: she does not possess the means, and it is *because* of her impotence that she is (or was) a 'wildcat'. Petruchio is not 'wild': he is simply taking literally the entitlement granted by civilization to the propertied to clout his servants into kingdom come and to the male to bring his wife to heel. While his manic exertions expose absurd excess, and thus may be read as self-parodying, the message to his wife and to the audience is an uncompromising endorsement of absolute power. And it is seen to work. Comic irony has Kate plead for that virtue so absent in her make-up and so requisite in women: patience, the prerogative of that paragon, Griselda, whom Petruchio has invoked in his wooing of this 'second Grissel' (II.1.288). 'Patience, I pray you, 'twas a fault unwilling,' she intercedes, and, when meat, 'trenchers, cups, and all' have been hurled at the servants (IV.1.151), she follows it up with another attempt to calm this living volcano:

> I pray you, husband, be not so disquiet.
> The meat was well, if you were so contented.
>
> (154–5)

These are the only words uttered by Kate in the scene. They recognize common cause with the servants, not only for the material reason that

Kate wants the warmth and dinner they can provide, but also because both classes are at the mercy of their lord. Addressing Petruchio as 'husband', she implicitly acknowledges his supremacy by the deferential 'I pray you' in both speeches and by addressing him by the formal 'you', as inferior to superior, rather than the intimate 'thou'. Save for the voluble and impertinent Grumio, the master's man, with whom Petruchio seems to enjoy verbal skirmishes, the household servants have no redress, whether in words or deeds. In Shakespeare's play, Christopher Sly has passed out long before these events, and the frame-plot cannot be brought into any significant relationship to the abused menials of the fourth act. When Petruchio bawls at Grumio for failing to produce his motley household of servants to greet his coming, he expresses himself incensed at the absence of his household retainers, who fall over themselves to present themselves for inspection:

ALL SERVINGMEN	Here, here sir, here sir.
PETRUCHIO	Here sir, here sir, here sir, here sir!
	You logger-headed and unpolished grooms!
	What, no attendance? No regard? No duty?
	Where is the foolish knave I sent before?
GRUMIO	Here sir, as foolish as I was before.
PETRUCHIO	You peasant swain, you whoreson malt-horse drudge!

(IV.1.109–15)

The names of the servants – the Nathaniel, Gabriel, Peter, Walter, Adam, Rafe and Gregory enumerated by Grumio – take us back from Padua to the world native to Sly – Marian Hacket, old John Naps, Peter Turph. The lower classes, together with Katherina in her denomination as Kate, have an Englishness that invites the audience to recognize them as country people. If Sly is on-stage watching, the scene will have more point, if little more hilarity for a modern audience, which tends to find the fourth act empty of humour. The degrading of the lower classes by insult and assault relates directly to Sly's experience. He too has been called the equivalent of an 'unpolished groom', a 'foolish knave', a 'peasant' and a 'drudge'. Theirs is a world he can comprehend, though in his present state of intoxication and illusion he relates to it from an aerial vantage point of gilded privilege.

If Sly has textually disappeared, as in the Folio version of *The Shrew*, such points of interaction will be entirely lost. However, in *A Shrew*, Slie is represented as avidly alert to the entertainment:

SLIE   *Sim*, when will the foole come againe?

LORD   Heele come againe my Lord anon.

SLIE   Gis some more drinke here, souns wheres
            The Tapster, here *Sim* eate some of these things.

LORD   So I doo my Lord.

SLIE   Here *Sim* I drinke to thee.

LORD   My Lord here comes the plaiers againe.

SLIE   O brave, heers two fine gentlewomen.

(A Shrew, p. 57)

The play's underlying conservative ideology focuses Slie's responses as those of a drunken peasant who has not the faintest idea as to how to rise to his lordly role. Through the murky haze of alcohol he seems to believe that he is still at the pub with Sim, his boozing companion. In any event, he is having the time of his life and wants more of it. He has especially relished the fool's (Sander's) contribution to the play, and goes on to act as gormless comic prologue to the next scene by mistaking Valeria in his music teacher's outfit for a woman ('O brave, heers two fine gentlewomen'). This has a multiple irony, since one of the two is a man, the other is that not very gentle woman, Kate (whose 'manhood' is later ironically noted by Aurelius), and both of course are played by boys. The presence of Slie would also serve to bring into relief Ferando/Petruchio's outrageous wedding garb, in which, turning the marriage ceremony into an anti-marriage in the central act, he profanes the sacred ritual, insults the community and shames his bride on her day of glory. In *A Shrew*, Kate expresses her sense of insult at the base clothing of her betrothed by wincing back in disgust from going to church 'with one so mad, so basely tirde,/To marrie such a filthie slavish groome' (p. 62). Expecting a presentable bridegroom, she finds a mucky stable-hand.

In the Shakespeare Folio, Kate is not present to receive and denounce her husband in his glad rags: she has already exited, weeping over the shame of his non-appearance, and her reactions are left to our imagination. For the wedding occurs off-stage, a non-event in terms of the action, though described by Gremio in graphic and berserk detail (III.2.156–82). It is important that the wedding should be a non-event, just as the wedding feast, which never takes place at all. For the central act witnesses the scold's punishment in a ritual of humiliation for Katherina. And the bridegroom's attire is an important element in this ritual. *The Shrew* draws attention to Petruchio's disrespectful wear by having him arrive late (thus building suspense as well as usurping the bride's prerogative of lateness to the altar), and then preluding his appearance by a long descriptive *tour de force* by Biondello, in which not only the groom's but his horse's and lackey's accoutrements are itemized (III.2.43–68): beginning with 'a new hat and an old jerkin; a pair of old breeches thrice turned; a pair of boots that have been candle-cases, one buckled, another laced . . .' (43–6). The horse, which can boast a full veterinary manual of diseases, is foully caparisoned, the servant being likewise 'caparisoned' (63) (a term used exclusively of horses). This disreputable and fantastic assemblage of incompatible articles of attire (new coupled with old, buckled with laced, stirrups that don't match, macho with female ('a woman's crupper')) expresses an asymmetry which in every detail declares that Kate's own refusal to pair conformably has brought this dishonour upon her. The outfit is meant not to define the wearer but to dangle a mocking mirror before the affronted eyes of the shrew. The implications of her disorderly conduct are manifest in these coupled incompatibles, which mar the match they proclaim and make odd what is expected to be even.

The asymmetry of Petruchio's gear is a version of the particoloured motley of the fool, who advertises his profession by opposing one side of himself to the other, and the whole of himself to the community, as a mocking mirror. Tranio, himself in a disguise which violates the dress code, inquires as to why Petruchio has appeared 'so unlike yourself' (103), presumably on the principle that it takes one to see one. Petruchio is of course playing the fool. Sly's presence on-stage, observing this orchestrated fiasco, would supply a perspective that includes a 'real' fool in borrowed clothes, reinforcing this costume chaos, and underscoring Petruchio's strategic abdication of class conventions. Gremio's use of the bridegroom/(stable)-groom pun (151–2) gives focus to the reversal Petruchio practises, in order to shame Kate. His actions deprive Katherina of a place in society until she is considered fit to occupy it. Bianca displaces her as centre of the feast: 'Lucentio, you shall supply the bridegroom's place,' says Baptista, 'And let Bianca take her sister's room' (248–9). For Kate is never truly married until, in the final act, she delivers a ritualized vow of love, honour and obedience to her husband in a public and ceremonious gesture of acquiescence. This in turn displaces Bianca (the new shrew) at her own marriage banquet. Thus, while Act III presents a theatrical version of the public humiliation of the scold who was carted through the streets, or 'ridden' in her bridle by jeering persons emitting rude and crude noises of ridicule, Act V releases the chastened Kate from the arena of public scorn into a version of the old marriage ritual as practised in pre-Reformation marriage rites in which, if lands accompany her dower, the bride 'prostrates herself at the feet of the bridegroom', or must 'kiss the right foot' of the husband (see Boose, p. 182). When Kate enjoins her fellow wives to 'place your hands below your husband's foot' and offers hers for this purpose (V.2.176–8), she embraces a position of spectacular public humility, exchanging this for the scold's humiliation of the central act, and completing her own marriage ceremony. However, in *A Shrew*, Slie misses this token of capitulation, for he has become comatose and been removed to awaken as his unaccommodated self, feeling the worse for wear and appealing to the Tapster in puzzlement, 'Am not I a Lord?' (p. 89).

No, *A Shrew* acknowledges, Slie is not and never was a lord, unless he can be seen, in the Tapster's sarcastic riposte, as 'A Lord with a murrin,' that is, a disease, or in this case probably a hangover or a screw loose. Slie was always part of the refuse at the bottom of the Elizabethan social heap, brought into dreaming relationship with the stars in the firmament in all their indifference and arrogance. Slie's re-emergence at the end of *A Shrew* sets back the whole preceding action into the realm of the fanciful, denying the solidity it has bodied forth. He is carried in 'in his one apparell againe' (p. 83), to be ditched where he had originally been found by the hunting party. At dawn when the Tapster arrives to trip over Slie's forgotten and oblivious body, he is awakened and declares the substance of his 'dreame': 'I know now how to tame a shrew' (p. 89). The Beggar rises less impotent than when he fell asleep, for whereas previously he had been wedded to his comforting bottle, now he is weaned on to the empowering knowledge that there is someone directly beneath him in the social heap, whom he now proposes to put in her place according to the code learned at the Petruchian taming school. Thus the perfect fantasies of art lead into the botched jobs and vulgar delusions of life.

5. Falconers and Falcons

Emily Brontë rescued a wounded merlin hawk from the moors above Haworth; in caring for the bird, she inadvertently tamed it, and grew to love it, naming it Hero. The beautiful picture she painted in 1841 of a hawk perched on a broken bough, standing erect and proud, on one foot with the other raised, talons retracted, may well be a life-study of Hero. The precision with which the geometry of the hooked beak, sharp eye and textured plumage is rendered respects the powerful otherness of the bird. A poem of the same year, entitled 'The Caged Bird', is a sombre testament of solidarity:

> Give we the hills our equal prayer:
> Earth's breezy hills and heaven's blue sea;
> We ask for nothing further here
> But our own hearts and liberty.
>
> Ah! could my hand unlock its chain,
> How gladly would I watch it soar,
> And ne'er regret and ne'er complain
> To see its shining eyes no more.
>
> But let me think that if to-day
> It pines in cold captivity,
> To-morrow both shall soar away,
> Eternally, entirely Free.

Emily Brontë's hawk stands as a proud affinity to her own nature, its chains the evidence of an impairment germane to the whole suffering creation. If paint on paper and words on a page may be said to reverence life, then it would be true to say that both picture and poem, dominated by the 'shining eyes' of the creature, reverence the inalienable otherness of the bird. The woman who affirms the right to be herself acknowledges a shared twofold need with the hawk, a need denied by the bondage of their parallel conditions: to possess 'our own hearts and liberty'. The speaker does not plunder or appropriate the creature's life but stands apart, alongside, comprehending its exile as she mourns her own. There is no question of either being capable of taming, which would insult both hawk and woman. In *Wuthering Heights* Emily

Brontë laments the male sport of 'devastating the moors' in a vision of bloodstained pastoral.

Shakespeare too was tender of hunted and suffering animals: one remembers the weeping stag of *As You Like It*. 'Come, shall we go and kill us venison?' says Duke Senior, but then, recalling man's invasive and carnivorous presence in the pastoral world of creaturely life, goes on:

> And yet it irks me the poor dappled fools,
> Being native burghers of this desert city,
> Should in their own confines with forked heads
> Have their round haunches gored.
> (*As You Like It*, II.1.22–5)

This is not the super-sensitivity of the over-civilized but a melancholy awareness of the universal 'penalty of Adam' in a fallen world (II.1.5). A wincing tenderness imaginatively experiences the shock as the shaft pierces the 'round haunches' of the deer. That feeling for creatures is there in *Measure for Measure* in regarding the pangs even of 'the poor beetle that we tread upon' (III.1.79) and in *Pericles* where the 'blind mole' tells 'the earth is thronged/By man's oppression, and the poor worm doth die for't' (I.1.101–3). But in *The Taming of the Shrew* this sensitivity is entirely lacking. The Lord and his retinue are hunters whose discussion of their hounds could serve as a hunting manual; Petruchio is a falconer who trains a woman for domestication according to the techniques prescribed in hawking lore. The audience is invited to taste the pleasures of the blood-sportsman's pursuit.

Men have from earliest times 'devastated' nature, formerly for food, latterly for sport, in Shakespeare's days for both; and hunting has always had a sexualized aspect. Its excitement roused the blood; the kill was a frenzied climax, which died into the carcase of deer or hare, boar or duck. Women could also be viewed as a kind of game, to be lured, trapped, baited, tracked, 'taken', spitted and ultimately devoured. Or, like wild animals for the use of man, they could be 'broken' or tamed. In *The Shrew*, Kate is first a shrew, then a hawk. To bring as movingly eloquent a poem as Emily Brontë's lyric for the hawk up against a comedy such as *The Shrew* may at first seem questionable in a complex of ways. After all, whereas her work is an elegy, Shakespeare's is a squib or jest. Two and a half centuries divide that man from this woman. Her heartfelt lament does not bear obvious comparison with his light-hearted entertainment. Yet I have chosen to align them because they expose, with a peculiarly dismaying nakedness, cultural assumptions that run deep into the patriarchal system of power-relations that determines conventional perception of how men and women, men and animals, and women and animals relate.

Jokes and comic antics may seem froth on the surface of culture, but what *makes* us laugh issues an imperative from the communal perception of what is 'natural' and 'normal' to the unguarded and, for the time being, uninhibited mind of the individual. Laughter can be provoked by the witty and aberrant; in more sinister fashion, it can be coerced. 'I couldn't help laughing,' we confess queasily. Feminists have often been reproached as killjoys for resisting the force of a mere joke. I myself have played a pained Malvolio in a group of male colleagues in a shout of laughter; and I have understood why they laughed, 'seen the joke' and perhaps have been tickled by it myself – and yet I could not join in. My gravity and their levity could not mate. Such complex problems are recorded by viewers of *The Shrew*:

The play seems written to please a misogynist audience, especially men who are gratified by sexually sadistic pleasures. Since I am outside the community for whom the joke is made and do not share its implicit values, I do not participate in its humor.

(Garner in Charney, p. 106)

As an outsider, it is possible to take a sceptical and serious look at the implications of the comedy. *The Shrew* makes an equation between woman and wild creature that authorizes and ritualizes sexual violence. Petruchio turns to the audience and in a memorable and graphic soliloquy explains his procedure:

> Thus have I politicly begun my reign,
> And 'tis my hope to end successfully.
> My falcon now is sharp and passing empty,
> And till she stoop she must not be full-gorged,
> For then she never looks upon her lure.
> Another way I have to man my haggard,
> To make her come and know her keeper's call,
> That is, to watch her, as we watch these kites
> That bate and beat and will not be obedient.
> She eat no meat today, nor none shall eat;
> Last night she slept not, nor tonight she shall not.
> As with the meat, some undeserved fault
> I'll find about the making of the bed,
> And here I'll fling the pillow, there the bolster,
> This way the coverlet, another way the sheets.
> Ay, and amid this hurly I intend
> That all is done in reverend care of her.

> And, in conclusion, she shall watch all night,
> And if she chance to nod I'll rail and brawl,
> And with the clamour keep her still awake.
> This is a way to kill a wife with kindness,
> And thus I'll curb her mad and headstrong humour.

> (IV.1.174–95)

The sexual implications of the procedure are focused in the verb 'to man'. In falconry a 'haggard' (an untrained fully-fledged hawk) was 'manned' by the technique of training that broke the autonomy of its will and bonded the bird to its master or keeper. In human sexual relations, the term 'haggard' was applied to a wayward or inconstant woman; 'manning' meant occupation of a vessel or control of a domain or colony, hence sexual possession or penetration, as in Donne's Elegie XIX, 'To His Mistress Going To Bed': 'My kingdome, safeliest when with one man man'd' (28). The language of falconry had long been incorporated into the discourse of sexual relations. Its scintillating dictionary of terms, methods and values implied mastery-as-affection, violent, caressive, extending the power of the man from earth to air. A hunting man invariably spoke of the quarry as 'she': 'he' hunts 'her'. A falconer could do the same with his falcon because the birds used in the sport were generally females, which are one third larger and stronger than males. A modern commentator says it all when he writes:

It is the only bird that can be tamed to achieve man's business without any link besides the tamed will. That taming sets up a special bond, having at times, apparently, a male–female relationship. It is itself the product of endless patience, understanding, and, in classical hawking, some cruelty.

(Henn, p. 24)

It is taken by this authority as axiomatic that human sexual relations naturally depend upon the subjugation of the female by the male and that 'patience' and 'cruelty' are compatible bedfellows in sport and sex. Petruchio's speech makes exactly the same assumptions.

Because the hawk was viewed as a majestic creature, a soaring precision killer, emblem of airborne pride, the prowess of taming it was all the greater because it was a genuine and elemental contest of wills. There could have been no such excitement in taming, for instance, a duck. The sexual thrill of *The Shrew* derives from and is dependent on the spirit and willpower of Kate. She is no 'easy lay'. Her resistance provides the dynamic allure to Petruchio's thrusting will. Petruchio maps out a procedure precisely equivalent to that of the falconers. Having caught his 'haggard' (married her), he will systematically starve her and deprive her of sleep until she surrenders. In Renaissance times hawks were fitted with jesses and varvels (straps to tie her to a perch or gloved wrist, with silver rings stamped with the owner's name). Then they were blinded by the sewing together of the eyelids (seeled), thus procuring maximum disorientation. Starved day and night and deprived of sleep, they would 'bate' (beat their wings) in their anguish on their perch, reaching a point of surrender. Some, as Petruchio notes, always remain 'kites/That bate and beat and will not be obedient,' but his 'kite'/Kate will not be one of these. When she breaks, she will break utterly. At this point, the hawk would be taught to sit on the master's wrist, be caressed and fed tidbits (tirings) from his hand, fly short distances attached by a créance (fine cord), to come to the 'lure' (meat on a string whirled around the master's head), and wear the hood and bells. By stages she would be entered upon prey such as small birds and rabbits, obeying the whistle in longer flights, and hovering motionless above the falconer's head, attending his will. Finally the keeper would fly his hawk in competition against other birds, and her victories would bring prestige to the owner.

The plot incorporates every element of the taming procedure. First she is caught: 'will you, nill you, I will marry you' (II.1.264). As soon as she has been labelled with her owner's name at the marriage ceremony, he begins his programme of starvation. The bride is denied her marriage feast. She 'bates' in fury: 'I will not go today,/No, nor tomorrow – not till I please myself' (III.2.207–8) but is removed to her cold perch in Petruchio's country house, where her lip begins to quiver as the food is snatched from under her very eyes:

KATHERINA   I pray you, husband, be not so disquiet.
                The meat was well, if you were so contented.
PETRUCHIO   I tell thee, Kate, 'twas burnt and dried away.

(IV.1.154–6)

The process of disorientation is carried further in the tedious business of the haberdasher and tailor, accompanied by the systematic refusal to hear anything Kate says until it is identical to the wish of her keeper. Finally, her hold upon reality is attacked, an equivalent of the seeling or hooding of the falcon:

PETRUCHIO   Good Lord, how bright and goodly shines the moon!
KATHERINA   The moon? The sun! It is not moonlight now.
PETRUCHIO   I say it is the moon that shines so bright.
KATHERINA   I know it is the sun that shines so bright.

PETRUCHIO   Now by my mother's son, and that's myself,
               It shall be moon, or star, or what I list,
               Or e'er I journey to your father's house.
               (*to the Servants*) Go on and fetch our horses back again.
               Evermore crossed and crossed, nothing but crossed!

                                      (IV.5.2–10)

It is at this point that Kate concedes. Sun is moon, aged man is young woman, if her dictator chooses to have it so. She will play his game in order to eat, sleep and move. The capitulation is completed when Petruchio receives his first 'voluntary' kiss. Kate now for the first time acknowledges her belonging to Petruchio by suggesting with timid eagerness a mutual course of action, addressing him as 'Husband':

KATHERINA   Husband, let's follow to see the end of this ado.
PETRUCHIO   First kiss me, Kate, and we will.
KATHERINA   What, in the midst of the street?
PETRUCHIO   What, art thou ashamed of me?
KATHERINA   No, sir, God forbid – but ashamed to kiss.
PETRUCHIO   Why, then, let's home again.
               (*to Grumio*) Come, sirrah, let's away.
KATHERINA   Nay, I will give thee a kiss.
               She kisses him
               Now pray thee, love, stay.
PETRUCHIO   Is not this well? Come, my sweet Kate.
               Better once than never, for never too late.

                                    (V.1.130–41)

Here is the brief turning-point at which Kate's submission turns to endearment. Now sour Kate is 'sweet Kate' indeed. This handful of lines has to be milked for all they are worth by an interpretation which wants to see Petruchio's courtship as consummated in the romantic bliss of mutuality. It has brought tears to the eyes of one apologist (see p. 54 above), who annotates thus:

Here, for the first time, there seems to be affection between the two, and the kiss seems a genuine expression of love. It is *possible* to play the lines as yet another example of Petruchio imposing his will on his unwilling wife, but to do so is to fly in the face of Shakespeare's obvious intention.

                         (Morris, Arden edn., p. 286, n.)

If Morris is right about 'Shakespeare's obvious intention' (and it is certainly feasible to play 'Why, then, let's home again' as a jokey retrospective and his 'never too late' as tenderly indulgent) this does not make the exchange less questionable. On the contrary, the echo only reinforces the play's reactionary endorsement of coercion and inequality as the basis of even companionate marriage. Kate has to be trounced before she can be espoused. The 'haggard' is 'manned' and can be 'flown'.

Bonding between hero and heroine in *The Shrew* is predicated on bondage. The falconers preened themselves on knowing the secret of brainwashing through a calculated mingling of gentleness with cruelty. 'Manning' the bird involved the construction of a 'love-relationship' (see Henn, p. 24) so that the bird became 'part of himself ... the subconsciousness of the man and the bird ... really linked by the mind's cord', in the sentimental and rhapsodic parlance of the author of *The Goshawk*, T. H. White (p. 37). He compares the man–hawk relationship with that of a mother and child, claiming that the falcon is 'created' out of part of the tamer's life. It would be a strange mother who sewed together her baby's eyelids. Renaissance manuals insist on the importance of caressing and stroking the bird as you break it. A seventeenth-century text, Blome's *Hawking or Faulconry*, suggests the keeper stroke the bird with a feather when it is docile. He lists techniques for making her 'very fond of you, full, haughty and proud' (p. 87). Gervase Markham's treatise 'Country Contentments' in his *A Way to Get Wealth* (1631–8) described the familiarization process thus:

All hawks generally are manned after one manner, that is to say, by watching and keeping them from sleep, by a continual carrying of them upon your fist, and by a most familiar stroking and playing with them ... and by often gazing and looking of them in the face, with a loving and gentle countenance, and so making them acquainted with man.

(pp. 36–7)

The most sinister factor in the analogy between hawk- and woman-taming is perhaps the eye contact by which the tamer extends to the object of his attentions the lure of a comforting emotion, in the midst of baffling her innate instinct for autonomy and freedom. When the falcon-woman has fallen for this bait, her will is effectively broken, and she ceases to belong to herself, having acknowledged the superiority *and* the lovability of her keeper. At this point the woman is co-opted into patriarchy, whose advocate she may become. Her tongue is put to use on behalf of the very values it had resisted, just as the falcon's predatory flight is co-opted to the use of the master species. In Act V, at the feast, Petruchio demonstrates to the marvelling company that

Kate will come at his 'whistle', without 'bating' and will 'stoop' to his command. In the wager scene, he 'flies' her, that is, he casts her up into her element and displays her resourceful use of her powers (the tongue) on his behalf, in competition with the 'haggards' of the rival husbands and to their chagrin. No sooner is the company settled at the table in the final act than the hyperactive Petruchio is itching to display his command, at the expense of his fellow husbands. The scene is a verbal and stylized equivalent of the jocular comparisons, at once penile and puerile, that we are told take place in the locker-rooms of squash clubs. Petruchio opens the contest by joshing Hortensio, 'Now, for my life, Hortensio fears his widow' (V.2.16); Kate, unbidden, proceeds to take on the widow in a round of sparring, while the respective husbands cheer on their partners:

PETRUCHIO   To her, Kate!
HORTENSIO   To her, widow!
PETRUCHIO   A hundred marks, my Kate does put her down.
HORTENSIO   That's my office.
PETRUCHIO   Spoke like an officer – Ha' to thee, lad.

(2.33–7)

Set at one another like a pair of fighting cocks, the two women are backed by their respective sponsors to put one another down. Hortensio's bawdy quibble (he is the right person to 'put down' his Widow, that is, on her back) reinforces the close tie between sex and power on which the drollery is based. The males jockey playfully for dominance in the hierarchy.

Petruchio next tries a skirmish with Bianca, whose riposte returns to the hunting metaphor. A man with a bow is hunting a bird in a bush; she will make herself scarce:

> Am I your bird? I mean to shift my bush,
> And then pursue me as you draw your bow.
> (46–7)

With the communal exit of the women, the field is now open to the males to bet on their prowess. A wager is proposed by Petruchio on which wife 'is most obedient,/To come at first when he doth send for her' (67–8). This wager, which often falls dismally flat in the theatre because of all the tramping and traipsing to and fro over the stage entailed by the summons and reply of the three women, makes little sense unless we recall the hawking metaphor. The obedience of the falcon to the whistle was *the* test of a bird's training. Demeanour when summoned was also significant. Petruchio here proves the completeness of his mastery in distinguishing Kate from 'these kites/That bate and beat and will not be obedient' (IV.1.181–2). 'What is your will, sir, that you send for me?' asks Kate demurely (V.2.99), coming to command without 'bating' and then instantaneously complying with the instruction to fly and fetch her recalcitrant fellow wives, using her tongue on them if necessary. At this display of Petruchio's success, Katherina's awed father adds an extra twenty thousand crowns to the dowry (112–27). Petruchio flaunts further, first getting Kate to throw her cap under his foot, to the execrations of the Widow and Bianca, who have now revealed themselves as 'froward', 'curst' and 'headstrong', taking Kate's place. As his final triumph, Petruchio sends his trained hawk soaring from his fist into her own element, that of language, an imperious and arrogant language ('Fie, fie, unknit that threatening unkind brow . . .' (135)), which is licensed as an extension of her master's control. While Kate's oration ironically violates the veto on female public speaking, it also assumes a higher rhetorical register than any other speech in the play as a miniature blank-verse treatise on the subjugation of the female, arguing from reason, natural law and political analogy to demonstrate women's natural inferiority as the basis of their duty of obedience. Couched as a rebuke to unduteous wives, the speech takes its relish from its authorized power to attack other women who were previously perceived as threatening to Katherina's status:

> I am ashamed that women are so simple
> To offer war where they should kneel for peace,
> Or seek for rule, supremacy, and sway,
> When they are bound to serve, love, and obey.
>
> (V.2.160–63)

> Come, come, you froward and unable worms,
> My mind hath been as big as one of yours,
> My heart as great, my reason haply more,
> To bandy word for word and frown for frown.
> But now I see our lances are but straws . . .
>
> (168–72)

The lofty 'I am ashamed . . .' has an elevated oratorical confidence that empowers the speaker to tower above her fellows, distinguishing her from the class among which she must number herself. Her contumacious verbal gesture 'Come, come' executes a pounce out of the sky of her own wit upon those 'unable worms' who murmur against their condition when they ought rather to grovel. Kate does not grovel: she displays her powers in oratory, commanding the stage for a conclusive solo performance. Her heart's desire is accorded her: to 'make a bondmaid and a slave' of her sister Bianca (II.1.2), tying if not her hands then her tongue, and striking her in the name of the law, while preening herself before the admiring male company. Kate can do this because she is 'manned' by Petruchio, demonstrating the truth of the old adage that women in their heart of hearts desire to be mastered by men whatever they assert to the contrary. In fact, the more they deny it, the more they 'really' want it. And the more resistance they put up, the stronger the sexual excitement for the man and the deeper the gratification of ultimate conquest: as witness the pleasured sigh of Petruchio after the speech, 'Why, there's a wench! Come on, and kiss me, Kate,' followed shortly by 'Come, Kate, we'll to bed' (V.2.179; 183).

There is never any question in *The Shrew* of Katherina making a symmetrical attempt to tame Petruchio. The question simply never arises. Shrews, hawks and wildcats are not, after all, people. Shrews may be a nuisance to people for, as Topsell wrote in his Renaissance bestiary, the creature is 'a ravening beast', which 'being touched it biteth deepe, and poisoneth deadly' for it 'beareth a cruell minde, desiring to hurt any thing' (*The Historie of Foure-footed Beasts* (1607), p. 536). Aggressive, sharp and screeching of voice, the animals indulge in shrill squeaking competitions to establish dominance. Their wickedness was proverbial and hence they fitted neatly into a scheme of thinking which saw a woman 'with lip' as a fiend. A shrew is no earthly use to anybody, nor would there be the slightest point in taming one, since the rodent cannot be used to any social advantage. Why does Shakespeare's play begin with a shrew and end with a falcon? In a strictly hierarchical universe, every created thing had its order and rank, reciprocally above someone and below somebody else, and whereas the shrew is a low-class animal by any standards, the falcon is the aristocrat of birds, the pet and pastime of princes, second cousin to the eagle, king of birds. Hence, Shakespeare has Petruchio graduate from small and noxious fry to the haughty paragon of the skies. Kate, who starts at ground level, excoriating all by nipping and screeching, ends by riding the air currents of sophisticated language and making her glamorous kills to pride the eye and ego of her keeper.

And, indeed, Petruchio did become a byword for woman-taming. The instant popularity of *The Shrew* and the fame of Petruchio are witnessed by the fact that John Fletcher wrote a reply to the play, *The*

Woman's Prize: or, The Tamer Tam'd, which was probably first acted in 1611. *The Woman's Prize* is one of the forgotten masterpieces of the period, which, had it been the work of Shakespeare rather than Fletcher, would no doubt still be produced regularly to packed houses. This sequel acts as a criticism of the values and fantasies incorporated in the original, and should ideally be read alongside *The Shrew*. It demythologizes and desexualizes the figure of Petruchio, who falls victim to his own conceit. Fletcher's play, which also resurrects Bianca and Tranio, opens after the death of Katherina, who, far from being tamed after the trouncing she received in *The Shrew*, led Petruchio such a life of it that even now (Tranio reports) he starts in his sleep, crying out for weapons to defend himself, 'Hiding his Breeches, out of feare her Ghost/Should walk, and weare 'em yet' (I.1.35–6). However, the widowed tartar, testy and brittle-nerved, has elected to marry again, a modest maiden named Maria. It is confidently predicted that Petruchio, who is so pathologically overbearing that the bride-to-be will be required to eat, drink and even piss to order, will kill the unfortunate young woman within three weeks. But Maria, stirred up by Bianca, shrugs off the warnings of those who know Petruchio (and, because his reputation is literary, this includes the audience) that ''Tis as easie with a Sive to scoop the Ocean/As to tame *Petruchio*' (I.2.105–6). For, announces the heroine,

> I am no more the gentle tame *Maria*;
> Mistake me not; I have a new soule in me
> Made of a North-wind, nothing but tempest;
> And like a tempest shall it make all ruins,
> Till I have run my will out.
>   (*The Woman's Prize*, I.2.70–74)

As the maiden prepares to launch herself against her partner, she represents herself in terms of incontrovertible natural energies, elemental forces monopolized by the rough-wooing Petruchio in *The Shrew*: 'Though little fire grows great with little wind,/Yet extreme gusts will blow out fire and all' (II.1.134–5). These 'extreme gusts', which in Shakespeare's play connote masculinity, are usurped by the whirlwind of Maria's initiatives, which in a dervish dance of improvisation and uppity creative humour, have the bridegroom reeling before every blast. In this reversal of gender-relations, Fletcher passes active initiative to Maria; Petruchio, floored, can only react defensively to the 'North-wind' of Maria's dazzling virtuoso sallies. He resorts increasingly to dolorous soliloquy; a moaning melancholic, he rants not against shrews but hedgehogs.

Indeed Maria is not a shrew, as he concedes. If she were a scold, whore or unthrift, he could control her because he could predict and pre-empt her. But she doesn't fit into any known category:

> A kinde of linsey woolsey mingled mischiefe
> Not to be ghest at, and whether true or borrowed,
> Not certaine neither . . .
>
> (IV.1.17–19)

> This woman would have made a most rare Jesuite,
> She can prevaricate on any thing . . .
>
> (55–6)

Maria's brilliant intelligence leads Petruchio a rampant dance, fighting not an individual but against a reputation and for a reputation of her own, founded on the defeat of his:

> You have been famous for a woman-tamer,
> And beare the fear'd-name of a brave wife-breaker:
> A woman now shall take these honours off,
> And tame you . . .
>
> (I.3.268–71)

In Fletcher's play, the women are not divided against one another but form a coherent subculture which unites against the males in a way reminiscent of Aristophanes' *Lysistrata*. All doors are 'barricadoed' against the men, who lay siege and battery against the rebels, led by Colonel Byancha, in the first act. In the second, the women consolidate their 'noble Cause/We now stand up for' (2.79–80), pledging in mock-heroic terms to found a new Amazon colony. The military rise of all the nation's womenfolk is led by a tanner's wife ('I know her by her hide' (II.4.42)) who enjoys the reputation of having flayed her husband in her youth and made 'Raynes of his hide to ride the Parish' (II.4.42–5). Petruchio, utterly unmanned, flounders in confusion: 'Come, something Ile do; but what it is I know not' (92). He laments his reputation and bewails the comedown of 'A wel known man of war' into an ass (II.5.8; 19). In the third act, Petruchio laments his barren wedding night, while Maria breezes about ordering new rich gowns and hangings, reversing Petruchio's sabotaging of her gown and cap in *The Shrew* (IV.3), and, complaining of the paltriness and 'ill air' of her new establishment, wonders whether it would be a good idea to have it completely demolished and rebuilt. Thereupon she executes the removal of all household goods and chattels, while having Petruchio locked up on the grounds that his ravings are symptoms of an infectious disease. In the fourth

act, Maria inveighs unctuously in martyred bitterness at his refusal to
have her near to comfort him in his sickness. The excoriated spouse
makes ready to threaten to leave England to escape this 'drench of
Balderdash', this 'strange carded cunningnesse', this rainbow woman
with her endlessly changing colours (IV.5.32–5). Maria now acts mute
and will under no circumstances be made to speak, exasperating Petruchio into undertaking to leave the country, at which she breaks forth
into an encomium, 'Go worthy man, and bring home understanding'
(153). Petruchio, who now finds himself in the position of having to set
sail, feigns dead before embarkation, only to have his wife utter the
epitaph, 'But let him rest,/He was a fool and farewell he' (V.4.30–31).
Finally he rises out of his coffin in a magnificently comic theatrical
gesture:

> Unbutton me,
> By Heaven I die indeed else. – O *Maria*,
> Oh my unhappinesse, my misery.
> (*The Woman's Prize*, V.2.39–41)

Maria relents:

> I have done my worst, and have my end, forgive me;
> For this houre make me what you please: I have tamed ye,
> And now am vowd thy servant.
> (44–6)

The tamed tamer's *crie de coeur*, representing emotional capitulation to
the person whose wit has aroused his fascination even as it defeated
him, is answered by a reciprocal gesture of self-surrender on the part of
his tamer.

Such reciprocity is never implied in *The Shrew*. Shakespeare's Petruchio lays down the law, not his arms, and if there is 'peace ... and
love, and quiet life' in store as he claims, that will be based on
'awful rule, and right supremacy', which he equates with 'what not
that's sweet and happy' (V.2.107–9). The dénouement of *The Woman's
Prize*, on the other hand, is genuinely touching because it derives
from a spasm of raw pain expressed in Petruchio's cry for Maria's
pity which, notwithstanding its utterance from a comic coffin, develops into a mutual accommodation of the pair to one another as
equals. This is explicit in the text, which undermines the misogyny of
The Shrew in equating female intelligence and spirit with sexuality
(Maria is the centre of attraction in the play), and affirming the
ideal of companionate marriage in the correspondence of equals.

The epilogue sums up this message: '*it being aptly meant,/To teach both Sexes due equality;/And as they stand bound, to love mutually*' (6–8). The point of the female rebellion against male tyranny is not to establish an alternative tyranny but to abdicate power-relations alto-gether by restoring the woman to her full stature. This theme is heralded in Maria's repudiation of the subjection of 'that childish woman' who forfeits her humanity 'and becomes a beast/Created for [man's] use, not fellowship' (I.2.138–9). 'Fellowship' is an important word, implying a common sharing and caring. When reminded that 'His first wife said as much' (that is, Shakespeare's Katherina), Maria ripostes dismissively, 'She was a foole' (136; 138–40) – all mouth and no action.

The text then launches straight into a reversal of Shakespeare's Petruchio's falcon speech (quoted on pp. 87–8 above), which presumably Fletcher expects his audience to have retained in memory:

MARIA Now thou comst neere the nature of a woman;
      Hang these tame hearted Eyasses, that no sooner
      See the Lure out, and heare their husbands halla,
      But cry like Kites upon 'em: The free Haggard
      (Which is that woman, that has wing, and knowes it,
      Spirit, and plume) will make an hundred checks,
      To shew her freedome, saile in ev'ry ayre,
      And look out ev'ry pleasure; not regarding
      Lure, nor quarry, will her pitch command
      What she desires, making her foundred keeper
      Be glad to fling out traines, and golden ones,
      To take her down again.

(*The Woman's Prize*, I.2.146–57)

This is how diminutive Petruchio appears from the vantage point of the high-riding falcon, disdaining his puny box of tricks (the 'Lure') and his ambition (the 'quarry'). Just as Shakespeare's Petruchio had glamourized his assertion of male domination by a display of technical terminology from falconry, so Fletcher's Maria replies in kind. She distinguishes the 'free Haggard' (the fledged and experienced young bird that has flown the nest) from 'tame hearted Eyasses' (an 'eyas' being the hawk caught as a helpless fledgling, lacking all its life in spirit and force, for it has been tamed by early bonding to the keeper). Maria's free and colloquial English expresses in every phrase relish for its com-mand and subversion of the traditional man-falcon symbolism for human gender-relations. Her virtuoso mastery of technical terminol-ogy (commended by her listener as 'learned' (157)) prides itself, as one who 'has wing, and knowes it,/Spirit, and plume'. The 'plume' is the name for the bird's feathers as used in flight and raised or ruffled in excitement, connoting pride in display, and suggesting the 'plumes' that, worn in head-dress or helmet, symbolized high rank and dignity in the social hierarchy. All such plumes, of course, are borrowed. While Petruchio may think of a wife as a feather in his cap, the woman's life and powers are in point of fact her own, part of her own self, and she 'knowes it'.

In falconry, the man controls the bird; from her bird's-eye view, Maria describes how beyond his control the bird actually is. She is airborne and he literally cannot reach her. Hence she makes successive 'checks', that is, false stoops when the hawk, forsaking the keeper's intended 'quarry', contradicts instructions and follows other game of her own choice. When she has reached a point of vantage (the 'pitch' being the height to which a falcon soars before swooping down on the prey), it is an elevation from which she can command 'What she desires.' The power-relation between keeper and creature is subverted by the will of the falcon, which engineers its own gratification at the expense (literally) of its 'foundred' (disabled or impotent) keeper, who is coerced into flinging out 'traines' (live birds attached to strings, or disabled birds set out to entice young hawks during training). But Petruchio will have to set out 'golden ones' before she will venture down, that is, Maria's nonchalant acquiescence will cost his pocket dearly.

Of course any falcon, like any wife, who openly behaved according to these principles of transgressive individualism, would soon in practice find herself on the scrap-heap. The 'free Haggard' (cant for a 'loose woman' or 'prostitute' in male usage, though without obscene connotation here) would be whistled off, disowned like Othello's Desdemona in that memorable image:

> If I do prove her haggard,
> Though that her jesses were my dear heart-strings,
> I'd whistle her off, and let her down the wind
> To prey at fortune.
>
> (*Othello*, III.3.257–60)

To be 'whistled off' was in practice a disaster for a woman, her state being dependent upon the goodwill of her keeper. Maria therefore expresses a fantasy of female autonomy. Petruchio in *The Shrew* enacts a fantasy of male power; but whereas his fantasy is sanctioned by society, hers represents an abdication of norms. Moreover, if Maria

99

accepts Petruchio's falcon metaphor, then however radically she subverts its implications, she still enrols herself among the colonized, the less-than-human by natural law. However waywardly the falcon manoeuvres, it is still in captivity. Maria accordingly drops the image immediately after this *tour de force*, and it does not control the management of the plot as in *The Shrew*. Setting herself against her exigent husband as a powerful adversary who fights on her own terms, in defiance of all the metaphors men have devised as agents of control, Maria vows:

> had this fellow tired
> As many wives as horses under him,
> With spurring of their patience; had he got
> A Patent, with an Office to reclaim us
> Confirm'd by Parliament . . .
> *(The Woman's Prize*, I.2.159–63)

> Or could he
> Cast his wives new again, like Bels to make 'em
> Sound to his will; or had the fearfull name
> Of the first breaker of wild women; yet,
> Yet would I undertake this man, thus single,
> And spight of all the freedom he has reach'd to,
> Turn him and bend him as I list, and mold him
> Into a babe again; that aged women,
> Wanting both teeth and spleen, may Master him.

BYANCHA Thou wilt be chonicl'd.

MARIA   That's all I aime at.

                                    (166–75)

Image-mongering Maria new-mints comparisons only to discard them, putting Petruchio in the saddle only to take his horse from under him; casting the bell of wifely obedience in the furnace of her own invention only to deprive it of chime. Abundant and abandoned metaphors scatter from her tongue as she charges into single-handed encounter: 'yet,/Yet would I undertake this man'. Significantly, she intends to make her victim 'a babe again'. The unacknowledged dependency which underlies the male power-drive, its bellicose but anxious need to master mother, is implied in *The Woman's Prize*, together with the fragility of the male ego when it is put to the test. In a play, as not in life, power is equated with power of speech, and it is because Petruchio can neither silence nor rival Maria's inventive and anarchic genius that he is worsted:

PETRUCHIO	She doth not talke I hope?
SOPHOCLES	Oh terribly, extreamly, fearfull, the noise at
	London-bridge is nothing neere her.
PETRUCHIO	How got she tongue?
SOPHOCLES	As you got taile, she was born to't.

(I.3.75–80)

Here is Fletcher's reworking of the notorious 'tongue in your tail' insult in *The Shrew*, in which Petruchio reinforces his sexual superiority by reminding Kate that his tongue is attached to a body whose phallic weapon is capable of putting her down in any contest of strength. Fletcher's Petruchio, who has taken a great pounding by female noise in his first marriage (at every meal a feast of 'ill language/Louder than *Tom* o'Lincoln' (III.2.158–9)), gets no advantage from his inheritance of 'taile'.

More than a decade and a half separates *The Shrew* from *The Woman's Prize*. While the greater sophistication of Fletcher's comedy reflects the evolution of drama in the hands of Shakespeare, Ben Jonson and a generation of Renaissance playwrights, its emotional maturity expresses not simply a provocative stab at accepted norms but some real if transient and ambiguous shift in consciousness within that period towards acknowledgement of women's desires and intelligence. But that re-valuation is built upon the ancient stereotype of woman's intemperate tongue, with intellect superadded. Lady Politick Would-Be in Jonson's *Volpone* emits a flux of noise which reduces the Fox in the midst of his stratagems to groaning impotence: 'Oh, oh, oh, oh, oh, oh!', while the Lady gibbers and jabbers away on arcane topics; and he must lie and seethe and listen:

> Oh,
> Rid me of this my torture, quickly, there;
> My madam, with the everlasting voice:
> The bells, in time of pestilence, ne'er made
> Like noise, or were in that perpetual motion!
> The Cock-pit comes not near it. All my house
> But now, steam'd like a bath with her thick breath,
> A lawyer could not have been heard: nor scarce
> Another woman, such a hail of words
> She has let fall. For hell's sake, rid her hence.

(*Volpone*, III.2)

Afflicted with that disease of the brain called femininity, Lady Politick is a newfangled Renaissance example of the old image of woman as mindless talker, her volubility garnished with berserk sprinklings of

Dante, Plato, Pythagoras. The norms that Fletcher's Maria subverts, Lady Politick endorses.

These outpoured rantings bring into relief the unacknowledged quiet of Kate and the uproar of Petruchio in Shakespeare's play. A carnivalesque figure who stands apparently ambivalently to the social order in his fierce energy and machismo, Petruchio actually endorses the establishment and its values. He irrupts like a geyser with sexual energy and confidence in the midst of the Paduan bidders and squabblers, but is essentially no different to them except in so far as he is able to imbue his search for lucre and standing with libido. He represents the buccaneering spirit of the adventurer out for both loot and excitement that won the Elizabethans colonies and markets, and his extravagant cavortings have a Marlovian flair, which covers up for their essential conservatism. Aggressive, go-getting, punchy and quarrel-picking, he is a lively alternative to the Paduan merchants and a down-to-earth ruffian in contrast to the romantic transports of Lucentio:

> Tranio, I burn, I pine, I perish, Tranio,
> If I achieve not this young modest girl.
> Counsel me, Tranio, for I know thou canst.
> Assist me, Tranio, for I know thou wilt.
>
> (I.1.152–5)

The mock-Marlovian diction of the romantic lover parodies itself in *The Shrew*: he loves his servant as Queen Dido of Carthage loved her maid, decorates his speeches with the fa-la of classical allusions, and sighs and dies for love with poetical lachrymosity. Petruchio enters in the next scene roughing up his servant, in an atmosphere of aggression and knockabout.

PETRUCHIO Villain, I say, knock me at this gate,
          And rap me well, or I'll knock your knave's pate.
GRUMIO My master is grown quarrelsome. I should knock you first,
          And then I know after who comes by the worst.
PETRUCHIO Will it not be?
          Faith, sirrah, an you'll not knock, I'll ring it.
          I'll try how you can *sol-fa* and sing it.
          He wrings him by the ears

                       (I.2.11–17)

'Villain', in general use as a term of insult, began life as the feudal villein, the landless peasant at the bottom of the social pile; 'knave' had a similar origin, meaning 'menial male servant', as opposed to knight.

Petruchio is first seen, therefore, driving home his inferior's inferiority by working him up to challenge it. Stirring him up, he talks and whacks him down, here by wringing the impertinent fellow by the ears as an encouragement to sing out in pain. To complete this less than hilarious joke, Petruchio rams home the point in the command, 'Now knock when I bid you, sirrah villain' (19). Both servant and master appear to enjoy this tussle, which characterizes the relationship between them throughout the play, and prefigures the assault on Kate. It becomes central again in the fourth act, at Petruchio's country house, in the master's abuse of the entire group of household servants.

The work of taming Kate is likened to the twelve labours of Hercules (I.2.254–5); and Hercules with his massive club and physical vitality is a fit patron for Petruchio's entrepreneurial methods, which tend to the ingenious but scarcely the subtle. He head-charges Padua, to its considerable surprise, bestriding the play as a self-declared colossus. In Act II, scene 1, at first meeting, he pounds Kate with the intimate form of her name:

PETRUCHIO   Good morrow, Kate – for that's your name, I hear.
KATHERINA   Well have you heard, but something hard of hearing;
            They call me Katherine that do talk of me.
PETRUCHIO   You lie, in faith, for you are called plain Kate,
            And bonny Kate, and sometimes Kate the curst.
            But Kate, the prettiest Kate in Christendom,
            Kate of Kate Hall, my super-dainty Kate,
            For dainties are all Kates, and therefore, Kate,
            Take this of me, Kate of my consolation –
            Hearing thy mildness praised in every town,
            Thy virtues spoke of, and thy beauty sounded,
            Yet not so deeply as to thee belongs,
            Myself am moved to woo thee for my wife.

(II.1.182–94)

'Kate' domesticates 'Katherine' by force; it impounds her. The impudence of making free with the familiar form of her name, not once or twice but eleven times in six lines, begets in the sexual sphere the playful aggression with which Petruchio took advantage of the servant at his first entrance. The virtuoso play on a gamut of 'Kates' provocatively conjures up a medley of roles for Katherina, all of his concoction. He promises meanwhile to eat her, for isn't she a 'cate' – a 'sweetmeat' – and hence a 'dainty', and not just dainty but 'super-dainty', being his to conjure with? Each repetition of 'Kate', agile, provocative, daft and

103

infuriating, hits the name's owner with her inability to hold on to herself. The bounding rhythms of the speech enact in language the performance Petruchio will stage as a sequence of violent and breathtaking theatrical events, taking over his wedding and its aftermath to universal astonishment. The initial repartee in which he forcibly 'Kates' Katherina is the verbal equivalent of a sexual dance of display, exhibiting his prowess and plumage as he rivets attention not only on himself but upon his intention to couple with her. Thus the outsider trespasses into Katherina's life, thrusting his bold face and quick tongue into her private space, breaching polite manners and social forms. Kate counters with asperity and some facility, sparking a quick give and take of ripostes which are sexualized by Petruchio's drive towards obscene innuendoes:

PETRUCHIO   Come, sit on me.
KATHERINA   Asses are made to bear, and so are you.
PETRUCHIO   Women are made to bear, and so are you.

(II.1.198–200)

The jokes tend towards Petruchio's reminder that he is in a position to penetrate Katherina, who is physically constructed to bear a man's weight; to be 'ta'en' like a dove by a buzzard (206–7); to have her waspish 'sting' drawn from her 'tail' (210–14). Here in the 'tongue in your tail' insult, the exchange peaks, with Kate maddened to the point of violent retaliation. Cock of the walk, Petruchio continues to display himself as her mate-to-be:

> For I am he am born to tame you, Kate,
> And bring you from a wild Kate to a Kate
> Conformable as other household Kates.
>
> (II.1.269–71)

It is important to recognize that the transgressive character of Petruchio is only skin-deep: it is a parodic medium through which he aims at the manufacture of a 'Kate/Conformable'. His nonconformity is in the service of 'family values' exemplified by the legion house-trained Kates who know their place and duty and whose depersonalization holds the social system together.

In the central act Petruchio turns up shamefully attired upon an ancient and decrepit horse and trailing an equally disgraceful servant; he knocks down the officiating priest at the wedding service and throws the sops from his ceremonial wine in the sexton's face, then he bundles his bride away from the untasted wedding feast. If there is an air of carnival about this one-man riot, where the sacred is deliberately profaned and due form and ritual violated, this inversion works to reinforce the norms. Saturnalia and other festive rituals including the Hocktide festivities (see Laroque, pp. 211–13) and the 'Lord of Misrule' ceremonies, which 'turned the world upside down', had a time-honoured social function of preserving the *status quo* by acting as a safety-channel for rebellious instincts. Shakespeare often drew upon these traditions of misrule for his festive comedies (see Barber). In his film of *The Shrew* (1967), Zefferelli replaced the Induction with a wild and orgiastic carnival procession. The anarchic energies of Kate and Petruchio, viewed in this light, reintegrated the society they appeared to challenge. Medieval festivals of misrule did not simply involve the travesty of the political and social order but also the authority of the Church, which was desecrated from within. One scandalized observer writing in Paris in 1445 complained of this sacrilege: 'priests and clerks are seen wearing masks and monstrous visages at the hours of Office: dancing in the choir, dressed as women, pandars, or minstrels, singing lewd songs. They eat black pudding . . .' (see Rossiter, p. 64). Thus, when the 'mad-brained bridegroom' replies to the priest's solemn question as to whether this man taketh this woman, with a hollered '"Ay, by gogs-wouns"' (that is, 'by God's wounds'), accompanied by a volley of oaths and succeeded by an assault on the priest (III.2.156–82), he is behaving in a manner true to the carnival spirit.

However, he is behaving thus *on his own*. For this reason, the idea of saturnalia is not as pertinent to this play as, for instance, to *Twelfth Night*. For carnival is a revel that involves either the whole community or a considerable section of it, a spree full of communal eating, drinking, dancing, singing, love-making and making merry. But Petruchio is a one-man show who aims to shock by standing out in exemplary fashion against the rules and codes by which society functions, and he inverts the rules of carnival in preventing eating, drinking and making merry. He has been compared with a Puritan, in his resistance to ritual and his avowed distaste for finery:

> To me she's married, not unto my clothes.
> Could I repair what she will wear in me
> As I can change these poor accoutrements,
> 'Twere well for Kate and better for myself.
> (III.2.116–19)

But this is nothing more than witty prevarication. Petruchio is no sober-suited Puritan but an outrageous parodist of Kate's resistance to the moral law. His mayhem is a comic extension of the implications of her refusal to co-operate with the established norms. Superficially he flouts authority, so that even Kate's less than adoring father takes her side ('such an injury would vex a saint,/Much more a shrew of thy impatient humour' (III.2.28–9)) and Tranio cautiously objects to the groom's 'unreverent robes' (111). But at the deepest level Petruchio's actions, even the most preposterous, assent to those norms and demonstrate their enforcibility. When he brings Baptista's daughter back to the paternal roof, he has done society's dirty work, in taking recalcitrant womanhood at its word as a threat to order and in demonstrating the consequences of disaffection and disorder in a mad, meatless, sleepless, unclad chaos. Petruchio acts out a comic version of the famous message of Ulysses in *Troilus and Cressida*:

> Take but degree away, untune that string,
> And, hark! what discord follows; each thing meets
> In mere oppugnancy: the bounded waters
> Should lift their bosoms higher than the shores,
> And make a sop of all this solid globe:
> Strength should be lord of imbecility . . .
> (*Troilus and Cressida*, I.3.109–14)

Kate, who is held to have spurned 'degree' and so far 'untuned that string' as to have broken his lute over the pate of her tutor, is taught by her wild mentor the meaning of 'discord', which is blared into her reeling ear night and day. Aghast, she implores her husband to be temperate in his dealings with the servants: 'Patience, I pray you, 'twas a fault unwilling'; 'I pray you, husband, be not so disquiet' (IV.1.142; 154) and is described as stunned into passivity: 'she, poor soul,/Knows not which way to stand, to look, to speak,/And sits as one new risen from a dream' (170–72).

In the 1993 production of *The Shrew* at the West Yorkshire Playhouse, Petruchio strode into the third act on stilts. Towering head and shoulders above the rest of the cast, he covered the stage in giant strides, while the puny Paduan people milled about beneath him. His belling green garb was sewn with multicoloured rags so that he resembled the totemic figure of the Green Man or a human maypole of colossal extension, a phallic fertility figure, funny and ridiculous but also imbued with all the dynamic menace of a natural energy. Kate stood on a table to contradict him, a small white-clad figure with one foot hobbled by a boot, for she was slightly lame, a sign of a handicap partly Oedipal but also social and emotional. She spoke back from this vantage point to the high-handed, tall-talking mocker:

Nay then,
Do what thou canst, I will not go today,
No, nor tomorrow – not till I please myself.
The door is open, sir, there lies your way,
You may be jogging whiles your boots are green.
For me, I'll not be gone till I please myself.

(III.2.206–11)

But her utmost tiptoe could not reach eye-level. Incommensurate, she had not the means of self-extension to compete with Petruchio's 'rope-tricks'; and he set her down on the floor with ease, and with scarcely a hint of wobble.

Select Bibliography

Primary works

Throughout this study the edition of *The Taming of the Shrew* primarily referred to is the New Penguin Shakespeare, edited by G. R. Hibbard (Harmondsworth, 1968), abbreviated to *The Shrew*. All quotations and line-references relate to this edition, except where otherwise stated. However, students wishing to study the play in detail for themselves are recommended also to use the Arden edition, edited by Brian Morris (London and New York, 1981) and the New Cambridge edition, edited by Ann Thompson (Cambridge and New York, 1984). All references to *A Pleasant Conceited Historie, called The Taming of a Shrew* are from the Harvester Wheatsheaf Shakespearean Originals edition by Graham Holderness and Bryan Loughrey (Hemel Hempstead, 1992), abbreviated to *A Shrew*.

Secondary Sources

Amt, Emilie (ed.), *Women's Lives in Medieval Europe: A Sourcebook*, New York and London, 1993.

Aristophanes, *Lysistrata*, A. H. Sommerstein (tr.), Harmondsworth, 1973.

Barber, C. L., *Shakespeare's Festive Comedy: A Study of Dramatic Form and its Relation to Social Custom*, Princeton, New Jersey, 1959.

Blome, R., *Hawking or Faulconry*, preface by E. D. Cuming, Facsimile of 1686 text, London, 1929.

Boose, Lynda E., 'Scolding Brides and Bridling Scolds: Taming of the Woman's Unruly Member', *Shakespeare Quarterly*, vol. 42, 1991, pp. 179–224.

Bradbrook, M. C., 'Dramatic Role as Social Image: A Study of *The Taming of the Shrew*', *Shakespeare-Jahrbuch*, vol. 94, 1958, pp. 132–50.

Caldwell, Patricia, *The Puritan Conversion Narrative: The Beginnings of American Expression*, Cambridge, 1983.

Cerasano, S. P. and Wynne-Davies, Marion (eds), *Gloriana's Face:*

Women, Public and Private, in the English Renaissance, New York and Toronto, 1992.

Charney, Maurice (ed.), *Bad Shakespeare: Revaluations of the Shakespeare Canon*, London and Toronto, 1988.

Darbishire, Helen (ed.), *Lives of the Early Milton*, London, 1932.

Dash, Irene G., *Wooing, Wedding, and Power: Women in Shakespeare's Plays*, New York, 1981.

Ezell, Margaret J. M., *The Patriarch's Wife: Literary Evidence and the History of the Family*, Chapel Hill and London, 1987.

Fell, Margaret, *Women's Speaking Justified*, 1667, Augustan Reprint Society, vol. 194, 1979.

Fletcher, John, *The Woman's Prize: or, The Tamer Tam'd* in *The Dramatic Works in the Beaumont and Fletcher Canon*, vol. 4, Fredson Bowers (ed.), Cambridge and London, 1979.

Fraser, Antonia, *The Weaker Vessel: Woman's Lot in Seventeenth-Century England*, London, 1984.

Garber, Marjorie, *Coming of Age in Shakespeare*, London and New York, 1981.

Garner, Shirley Nelson, '*The Taming of the Shrew*: Inside or Outside of the Joke' in Charney, Maurice (ed.), *Bad Shakespeare: Revaluations of the Shakespeare Canon*, London and Toronto, 1988.

Goddard, Harold C., *The Meaning of Shakespeare*, Chicago, 1951.

Hannay, Margaret Patterson, *Silent but for the Word: Tudor Women as Patrons, Translators and Writers of Religious Works*, Kent, Ohio, 1985.

Haring-Smith, Tori, *From Farce to Metadrama: A Stage History of 'The Taming of the Shrew', 1594–1983*, Westport and London, 1985.

Hazlitt, W. C., *The English Drama and Stage: Documents Relating to Theatres*, London, 1869.

Henn, T. R., *The Living Image: Shakespearean Essays*, London, 1972.

Hillman, Richard, *Shakespearean Subversions: The Trickster and the Play-text*, London and New York, 1992.

Hogrefe, Pearl, *Tudor Women: Commoners and Queens*, Ames, Iowa, 1975.

— *Women of Action in Tudor England: Nine Biographical Sketches*, Ames, Iowa, 1977.

Holderness, Graham, '*The Taming of the Shrew*': *Shakespeare in Performance*, Manchester and New York, 1989.

— (ed.), *The Shakespeare Myth*, Manchester, 1988.

Huston, J. D., *Shakespeare's Comedies of Play*, New York, 1981.

Critical Studies: The Taming of the Shrew

Kahn, Coppelia, *Man's Estate: Masculine Identity in Shakespeare*, Berkeley, Los Angeles and London, 1981.

Laroque, François, *Shakespeare's Festive World: Elizabethan Seasonal Entertainment and the Professional Stage*, 1988, Janet Lloyd (tr.), Cambridge and New York, 1991.

Levith, Murray J., *Shakespeare's Italian Settings and Plays*, Basingstoke and London, 1989.

Maclean, Ian, *The Renaissance Notion of Woman: A Study in the Fortunes of Scholasticism and Medical Science in European Intellectual Life*, Cambridge and London, 1980.

Markham, Gervase, 'Country Contentments' in *A Way to Get Wealth*, 1631–8.

Marowitz, Charles, *Recycling Shakespeare*, Basingstoke and London, 1991.

Marshall, Norman, *The Producer and the Play*, London, 1962.

Marshall, Rosalind K., *Virgins and Viragos: A History of Women in Scotland from 1080 to 1980*, London, 1983.

Marshall, Sherrin (ed.), *Women in Reformation and Counter-Reformation Europe: Private and Public Worlds*, Bloomington and Indianapolis, 1989.

Moisan, Thomas, '"Knock me here soundly": Comic Misprision and Class Consciousness in Shakespeare', *Shakespeare Quarterly*, vol. 42, 1991.

Nevo, Ruth, *Comic Transformations in Shakespeare*, London, 1980.

O'Faolain, Julia and Martines, Laura, *Not in God's Image*, London, 1973.

Parker, Patricia and Hartman, Geoffrey (eds.), *Shakespeare and the Question of Theory*, New York and London, 1986.

Rossiter, A. P., *English Drama from Early Times to the Elizabethans*, New York, 1967.

Slater, Ann Pasternak, 'An Interview with Jonathan Miller', *Quarto*, vol. 10, 1988.

Spenser, Edmund, *The Faerie Queene*, J. C. Smith and E. de Selincourt (eds.), London, New York and Toronto, 1912.

Stone, Lawrence, *The Family, Sex and Marriage, 1500–1800*, Harmondsworth, 1979.

Tan, Amy, *The Kitchen God's Wife*, London, 1991.

White, T. H., *The Goshawk*, London, 1951.

Winter, William, *Shakespeare on Stage*, Second Series, New York, 1915.

Woodbridge, Linda, *Women and the English Renaissance: Literature and the Nature of Womankind, 1540–1620*, Urbana and Chicago, 1986.

Discover more about our forthcoming books through Penguin's FREE newspaper...

Penguin Quarterly

It's packed with:

- exciting features
- author interviews
- previews & reviews
- books from your favourite films & TV series
- exclusive competitions & much, much more...

Write off for your free copy today to:
Dept JC
Penguin Books Ltd
FREEPOST
West Drayton
Middlesex
UB7 0BR
NO STAMP REQUIRED

READ MORE IN PENGUIN

In every corner of the world, on every subject under the sun, Penguin represents quality and variety – the very best in publishing today.

For complete information about books available from Penguin – including Puffins, Penguin Classics and Arkana – and how to order them, write to us at the appropriate address below. Please note that for copyright reasons the selection of books varies from country to country.

In the United Kingdom: Please write to *Dept. JC, Penguin Books Ltd, FREEPOST, West Drayton, Middlesex UB7 0BR.*

If you have any difficulty in obtaining a title, please send your order with the correct money, plus ten per cent for postage and packaging, to *PO Box No. 11, West Drayton, Middlesex UB7 0BR*

In the United States: Please write to *Consumer Sales, Penguin USA, P.O. Box 999, Dept. 17109, Bergenfield, New Jersey 07621-0120.* VISA and MasterCard holders call 1-800-253-6476 to order all Penguin titles

In Canada: Please write to *Penguin Books Canada Ltd, 10 Alcorn Avenue, Suite 300, Toronto, Ontario M4V 3B2*

In Australia: Please write to *Penguin Books Australia Ltd, P.O. Box 257, Ringwood, Victoria 3134*

In New Zealand: Please write to *Penguin Books (NZ) Ltd, Private Bag 102902, North Shore Mail Centre, Auckland 10*

In India: Please write to *Penguin Books India Pvt Ltd, 706 Eros Apartments, 56 Nehru Place, New Delhi 110 019*

In the Netherlands: Please write to *Penguin Books Netherlands bv, Postbus 3507, NL-1001 AH Amsterdam*

In Germany: Please write to *Penguin Books Deutschland GmbH, Metzlerstrasse 26, 60594 Frankfurt am Main*

In Spain: Please write to *Penguin Books S. A., Bravo Murillo 19, 1° B, 28015 Madrid*

In Italy: Please write to *Penguin Italia s.r.l., Via Felice Casati 20, I–20124 Milano*

In France: Please write to *Penguin France S. A., 17 rue Lejeune, F–31000 Toulouse*

In Japan: Please write to *Penguin Books Japan, Ishikiribashi Building, 2–5–4, Suido, Bunkyo-ku, Tokyo 112*

In Greece: Please write to *Penguin Hellas Ltd, Dimocritou 3, GR–106 71 Athens*

In South Africa: Please write to *Longman Penguin Southern Africa (Pty) Ltd, Private Bag X08, Bertsham 2013*

READ MORE IN PENGUIN

CRITICAL STUDIES

Described by *The Times Educational Supplement* as 'admirable' and 'superb', Penguin Critical Studies is a specially developed series of critical essays on the major works of literature for use by students in universities, colleges and schools.

Titles published or in preparation include:

The Poetry of William Blake
Dickens' Major Novels
Doctor Faustus
Emma and Persuasion
Great Expectations
The Great Gatsby
Heart of Darkness
The Poetry of Gerard
  Manley Hopkins
Joseph Andrews
Jude the Obscure
The Poetry of Keats
Mansfield Park
The Mayor of Casterbridge
The Metaphysical Poets
Middlemarch
The Mill on the Floss

Milton: The English Poems
The Portrait of a Lady
A Portrait of the Artist as a
  Young Man
The Return of the Native
Rosencrantz and Guildenstern
  are Dead
Sense and Sensibility
The Poetry of Shelley
Sons and Lovers
Tennyson
Tess of the D'Urbervilles
To the Lighthouse
The Waste Land
Wordsworth
Wuthering Heights
The Poetry of W. B. Yeats

READ MORE IN PENGUIN

CRITICAL STUDIES

Described by *The Times Educational Supplement* as 'admirable' and 'superb', Penguin Critical Studies is a specially developed series of critical essays on the major works of literature for use by students in universities, colleges and schools.

Titles published or in preparation include:

SHAKESPEARE

Antony and Cleopatra
As You Like It
Coriolanus
Henry IV Part 2
Hamlet
Julius Caesar
King Lear
The Merchant of Venice
A Midsummer Night's Dream
Much Ado About Nothing
Othello
Richard II
Richard III
Romeo and Juliet
Shakespeare – Text into Performance
Shakespeare's History Plays
The Tempest
Troilus and Cressida
Twelfth Night
The Winter's Tale

CHAUCER

Chaucer
The Pardoner's Tale
The Prologue to The
   Canterbury Tales

READ MORE IN PENGUIN

THE NEW PENGUIN SHAKESPEARE

All's Well That Ends Well	Barbara Everett
Antony and Cleopatra	Emrys Jones
As You Like It	H. J. Oliver
The Comedy of Errors	Stanley Wells
Coriolanus	G. R. Hibbard
Hamlet	T. J. B. Spencer
Henry IV, Part 1	P. H. Davison
Henry IV, Part 2	P. H. Davison
Henry V	A. R. Humphreys
Henry VI, Parts 1–3	Norman Sanders
(three volumes)	
Henry VIII	A. R. Humphreys
Julius Caesar	Norman Sanders
King John	R. L. Smallwood
King Lear	G. K. Hunter
Love's Labour's Lost	John Kerrigan
Macbeth	G. K. Hunter
Measure for Measure	J. M. Nosworthy
The Merchant of Venice	W. Moelwyn Merchant
The Merry Wives of Windsor	G. R. Hibbard
A Midsummer Night's Dream	Stanley Wells
Much Ado About Nothing	R. A. Foakes
The Narrative Poems	Maurice Evans
Othello	Kenneth Muir
Pericles	Philip Edwards
Richard II	Stanley Wells
Richard III	E. A. J. Honigmann
Romeo and Juliet	T. J. B. Spencer
The Sonnets *and* A Lover's Complaint	John Kerrigan
The Taming of the Shrew	G. R. Hibbard
The Tempest	Anne Barton
Timon of Athens	G. R. Hibbard
Troilus and Cressida	R. A. Foakes
Twelfth Night	M. M. Mahood
The Two Gentlemen of Verona	Norman Sanders
The Two Noble Kinsmen	N. W. Bawcutt
The Winter's Tale	Ernest Schanzer